MICHAEL HUTTON-WOOD

WHAT IS MINISTRY?

[WHAT IT IS AND WHAT IT ISN'T]

hwp

Unless otherwise indicated, all scriptural references are taken from the King James Version of the Bible.

WHAT IS MINISTRY?
ISBN 978-0-9562541-0-8
Copyright © MAY 2011 by Michael Hutton-Wood
Hutton-Wood Publications

In the UK write to:
Michael Hutton-Wood Ministries
P. O. Box 1226, Croydon. CR9 6DG.
Or in the UK
Call: Tel. 020 8689 6010; 07956 815 714
Outside the UK call: +44 20 8689 6010; +44 7956 815 714
Or contact: WEBSITE: www.houseofjudah.org.uk

Email:
michaelhutton-wood@fsmail.net
houseofjudah@ymail.com
leadersfactoryinternational@yahoo.com

Published & distributed by:
Michael Hutton-Wood Ministries
(Incorporating Hutton-Wood World Outreach Ministries)

All rights reserved under international copyright law. Written permission must be secured from the publisher to use or reproduce any part of this book.

Printed in the United Kingdom

THE MANDATE

'...SET IN ORDER THE THINGS THAT ARE OUT OF ORDER AND RAISE AND APPOINT LEADERS IN EVERY CITY.'
- Titus 1:5

MICHAEL HUTTON-WOOD MINISTRIES
RELEASING POTENTIAL
- MAXIMIZING DESTINY

HOUSE OF JUDAH (PRAISE) MINISTRIES
&
LEADERS FACTORY INTERNATIONAL
RAISING GENERATIONAL LEADERS
- IMPACTING NATIONS

CONTENTS

Introduction		7
Ministry Nuggets: 35 Life-Changing Statements To Expect In This Book		9
1	What Is Ministry?	15
2	17 Fundamental Laws For Fulfilling Your Ministry	54
3	45 Additional Prescriptions For Fulfilling Your Ministry	121
4	Failure-Proofing Your Ministry Through The Force Of Faith	130
5	Adopting A Zero-Tolerance For Discouragement In Ministry	159
6	Securing Your Enviable Place In History Through Selflessness: [The Capital Price For Impactful Leadership]	168

A need is not equal to a calling on your life.
That there is a need is not equal to a calling on your life.
There are needs every day.
An open door is not equal to an open vision.

INTRODUCTION

What many think ministry really is or is about, is not what it is at all. Some are entering ministry today for all kinds of reasons: some because of money, fame, wealth, failed careers, talents, need, lack, appointments by men based on eloquence, gifts or charisma, etc. thinking it's a way of making cheap money or captured by the glory they see without settling down to understand the story behind the glory. This book has been written to quash those myths and ideas some have so they don't make a shipwreck of both their faith and life and destroy both their lives and those who may follow them in rebellion or out of ignorance and in the simplicity of their minds like those who followed Absalom and paid for the consequences of rebellion as recorded in 2 Samuel 15:11-12, 'And with Absalom went two hundred men out of Jerusalem, that were called; **and they went in their simplicity, and they knew not any thing.** And Absalom sent for Ahithophel the Gilonite, David's counsellor, from his city, even from Giloh, while he offered sacrifices. And the conspiracy was strong; for the people increased continually with Absalom.'

IN THE KINGDOM, IGNORANCE IS NOT AN EXCUSE!

What we all need to realize is: as to how you entered ministry whether you were aware of it or not, or knew or did not know does not exempt you from stripes as Jesus made categorically clear in Luke 12:47-48, '**And that servant, which knew his lord's will, and prepared not himself, neither did according to his will, shall be beaten with many stripes. But he that knew not, and did commit things worthy of stripes, shall**

be beaten with few stripes. For unto whomsoever much is given, of him shall be much required: and to whom men have committed much, of him they will ask the more.'

Calling yourself into ministry or someone appointing you into ministry or you by your own 'wise self' entering ministry without understanding the true intricacies and dynamics of ministry is a self-inflicted curse and tantamount to a life of unending frustration and struggles not only for you but your family, rebellious followers or 'poor' 'innocent' ones who in the simplicity of their minds followed you or appointed you as their leader. So, it is imperative that we find out what ministry really is and what it isn't so we don't make a shipwreck and a nuisance of both our faith and that of those who follow us, abuse them and end up derailing and destroying countless destinies. **That is the essence of this book birthed from my leadership training manual, MINISTRY 101.**

LIFE-CHANGING STATEMENTS TO EXPECT IN THIS BOOK

1. Embarking on a Ministry without a clear call, empowerment and certified sending is equivalent to madness and is a self-inflicted curse. I repeat: It is a self-inflicted curse to embark on any ministry enterprise that God did not call you to embark on.

2. Calling yourself into ministry is madness of the highest order.

3. IN THE KINGDOM, COMMON SENSE IS NONSENSE!

4. IN THE KINGDOM, IGNORANCE IS NOT AN EXCUSE! If you enter ministry without a call or because it looks inviting or out of a need, whether you were aware of it or not, whether you know or did not know does not exempt you from stripes as Jesus said in Luke 12:47-48, 'And **that servant, which knew his lord's will, and prepared not himself, neither did according to his will, shall be beaten with many stripes. But he that knew not, and did commit things worthy of stripes, shall be beaten with few stripes.** For unto whomsoever much is given, of him shall be much required: and to whom men have committed much, of him they will ask the more.'

5. **God will only finance what He commands you to embark on**. (Lamentations 3:37; Luke 22:35)

6. **WHEN DIVINITY COMES UPON HUMANITY IT RELEASES AN UNCOMMON PERSONALITY.**

7. **The statement: 'WRITE THE VISION DOWN' in Habakkuk 2 means: Describe it, Inscribe it, Prescribe For it and Subscribe To it.**

8. Making the most of your time is making the most of your life and ministry. (1 Thessalonians 4:11) Wasting the most of your time is wasting the most of your life and ministry.

9. Divine appointments avert severe disappointments. (Lamentations 3:37) Divinely-sent people triumph by God's hand. (2 Corinthians 2:14)

10. Venturing into someone's assignment can kill you.

11. Ministry is running and preaching His message, not your message.

12. The next move of God in your life is entirely up to you. Discard the doctrine of waiting for God He is waiting for you to 'pay the price'.

13. If He called you, He will do it, but if He did not call you then you will do it.

14. Ministry is a tongue baptized with fire [not noise]. - Isaiah 6:6-8

15. Ministry is about being a news-maker not a noise-maker.

16. Ministry is: Knowing and being persuaded of if you are called, why you are called, who you are called to, where you are called, to whom you are called, when to step out, what you are called to do and say, staying where you are called and knowing how to accomplish your calling. BE AND GO WHERE HE TOLD YOU TO BE/GO, DO ONLY WHAT HE TOLD YOU TO DO AND STAY WHERE HE TOLD YOU TO STAY.

17. Ministry is what you are within you not what is on the outside. It is the transaction of covenant.

18. Ministry is not a popularity contest.

19. Ministry is not initially about you being famous but making Him known and famous and in the process of you exalting, lifting, glorifying Him and making Him known, you also become known because of Him. As confirmed in the following passage: John 12:32, 'And I, if I be lifted up from the earth, will draw all men unto me.'

20. The foundation for a successful ministry is not your eloquence – it is emphatically your divine calling.

21. Ministry begins with and is sustained by a heavenly calling. **In ministry there is no such thing as luck. If you are not heavenly-called, you have no heavenly backing and if you don't have heavenly backing, you are an easy target exposed to the gates of hell prevailing against you and even angels cannot help you.**

22. Ministry requires daily consultation with your Caller for clear, divine instructions that secure undisputed, maximum and lasting supernatural results. Your creativeness/creativity and innovation in ministry must be accompanied by and subjected to daily consultation with the Holy Spirit [the owner of the Church] for approval and divine direction. **In every endeavour, learn to submit your creativity to Divinity for instruction, approval, empowerment, correction or adjustment.**

23. STOP INVITING GUEST SPEAKERS ON AN ONGOING BASIS TO MILK, HARASS AND ERAZE YOUR MEMBERS BY RAISING AND RAISING OFFERINGS THROUGH CARNAL, MARKETING AND PUBLIC RELATIONS STRATEGIES. A LASTING CHURCH IS NOT BUILT ON GUEST SPEAKERS.

24. The strength of your ministry and the guarantee of your supplies lie in the depth of your commitment to your core assignment. (Luke 8:1-3; 22:35) The strength of any ministry therefore is not in its spread, but in its depth; so preach the Word in season and out of season. (2 Timothy 4:2) Do not let anything or anyone take you off your core assignment because that is what determines your overall success in ministry.

25. Ministry essentially means a minister bearing a message that meets the needs of mankind through the instrumentality of the Word.

26. Preaching the Word is what makes ministry and ministry is what makes money. The WORD is what determines

the quality of your ministry which in turn determines the quality of life you enjoy.

27. Ministry is not just a commitment; it is a commission.

28. Ministry is a divine appointment not a self-appointment.

29. Ministry demands a definite and clearly-defined message – that is the core assignment of one's ministry.

30. At the centre of every great ministry is the Word.

31. No matter the needs of your ministry, God has all it takes to meet them all. **Your resources are not in the hands or pockets of men but in His hands. Human sponsors hijack or limit your ministry.**

32. Behind every successful ministry is a successful family life.

33. The level of opposition you face in ministry shows your strong position.

34. The reality of an Open heaven over a ministry/church requires the Pastor to be a covenant practitioner – i.e. to be a tithing and giving Pastor and the ministry to remain a tithing and giving ministry/church.

35. Ministry is impossible without the anointing. (Isaiah 11:1-3; Zechariah 4:6-7)

1

MINISTRY
What it is and what it isn't.

BEHIND EVERYTHING OUTSTANDING IS UNDERSTANDING! Therefore, an initial understanding of these classifications will give us a better approach and the right perspective towards ministry.

CLASSIFICATION OF MANAGEMENT SYSTEMS
- 3 classes
i. Managing people or people-management is Organization
ii. Resource management is Administration
iii. Destiny Management is Ministry

So: Ministry unlike organisation and administration is about people's destinies. It is imperative therefore that we have a clear understanding of what ministry is before stepping out so we don't end up destroying our lives, families and destinies entrusted or not entrusted to us. **At The root of everything outstanding is understanding!**

1. Ministry begins with discovering your Source and is sustained by continuous communication with your Source - God. - Jeremiah 1; 29:11

2. Ministry begins with self-discovery - a discovery of your self - who and what you really are and adequate and relevant preparation. - Jeremiah 1

3. Ministry begins with a purposeful discovery of your purpose in life – why you are here and what you are called to do. (Pastor, Evangelist, Apostle, Prophet or Teacher)

4. Ministry begins with a discovery, clear understanding and appreciation of your passion, gifts and talents - knowing what you are passionate about and your wiring i.e. why you're wired the way you are – potential.

5. Ministry begins with a discovery, recognition and clear understanding of your strengths, weaknesses and operating the law of compensation.

6. Ministry therefore is about people's destinies and fulfilling vision which comes through a discovery of your Source, your purpose, yourself, your gifts, talents, strengths and maximizing opportunities made possible by:
a.　Fellowship in prayer with the Holy Spirit to introduce you to you, for an understanding of you - yourself - why you are 'wired' the way you are, to discover your assignment in life [purpose], your potential – your capabilities –

gifting [gifts/talents], strengths / weaknesses.
b. Asking God for wisdom and engaging in spiritual warfare
c. Having clarity of vision and pursuing it vigorously/ diligently
d. Addiction to The Word – This book of the Law should never depart out of your mouth; it should be your meditation all day long and be the final arbiter of your life/destiny (Joshua 1:8; Psalm 119:97-100)
e. Knowing the following six crucial points: The 'who', the 'what', the 'way', [the how] the 'why', the 'when', and the 'where'. Rudyard Kipling said: "I keep six honest serving men (They taught me all I knew); Their names are What and Why and When And How and Where and Who."

SO MINISTRY BEGINS WITH KNOWING THE WHO, THE WHAT, THE WAY, [the how] THE WHY, THE WHEN AND THE WHERE!

a. THE WHO: Who is the target? Who are you called to? Who is to be involved? Genesis 11:6, '….and the people is one; nothing will be restrained from them which they have imagined to do' & 2 Samuel 6. Also, with whom are you to fulfil destiny since you are not called to serve with everyone. Paul to the Gentiles (Acts 26:14-19) recommended and supported by Barnabas, Luke, Timothy, Titus; Peter to the Jews.

b. THE WHAT: What is the assignment? What is the target? And all this must reflect His image and bring Him glory. That of Nimrod and those in Babel was nullified because it was for self - self-aggrandisement; it was aimed at bringing them the glory and not God. That is why God came down and interrupted their program.

c. THE WAY: [how to achieve it] In 2 Samuel 6, King David initially employed the wrong way to carry or bring the ark back to Jerusalem; there was a prescribed way as stated in 1 Samuel 5-7 which should have been studied by David the king before employing natural, physical, trial and error means using a cart to transport the ark resulting in Uzzah in trying to stop the ark from falling by touching it – helping God, being killed. King David eventually repented, wised up, found and followed the right way to bring the ark back. Find the divinely prescribed way or you'll end up using a blunt axe, exerting human effort and energy to accomplish little [Ecclesiastes 10:10] wearing everyone out or even killing yourself or others. Hebrews 8:5 says, '.....See, saith he, that thou make all things according to the pattern showed to thee in the mount.'

d. THE WHY: Why did God give you the vision you have? Why are you doing what you are doing? Why did He give you that assignment? Moses was told tell Pharaoh, 'Let my people go [why?] That they may serve me, worship me and sacrifice to me in the wilderness.' (Exodus 4, 8, 9,)

1 Kings 3:5-9, 'Give me an understanding heart' – Why? Not for me but that I may be able to judge thy so great a people.

There is always a 'why' to everything God asks you to do - find it. It helps make the journey great and significant producing maximally with ease and keeps you focussed when others doubt and criticise you.

- Hebrews 12:2 says, '… Jesus, who for the joy that was set before him, endured the cross, despised the shame and is now set at the right hand of majesty.'

Why are we here?

Genesis 2:5, 'And every plant of the field before it was in the earth, and every herb of the field before it grew: for the LORD God had not caused it to rain upon the earth, and there was not a man to till the ground. But there went up a mist from the earth, and watered the whole face of the ground.'

There was no rain because there was no man to till the ground. There is always a reason for everything that God does. If certain things are not in place God doesn't do certain things because there is time for everything as stated in Ecclesiastes 3.

In Genesis 2:5-6, because, there was no man to till the ground God sent a mist out of the ground to water the ground.

e. THE WHEN: There is a when to every vision that God gives to every man. [Habakkuk 2 – though the vision tarries, wait for it, for it shall surely come to pass]. E.g. Esther in the palace; Moses in the wilderness with Jethro – the Midianites; David in the wilderness; Joseph sold into slavery ending up in prison for the preservation of life [posterity] - Ecclesiastes 3:1-3. The timing and environment must be right for the manifestation of the vision. Finding the when makes all the difference and takes the sweat out of life. In the fullness of time, God sent his Son.

f. THE WHERE: Where is God going to bring the promise to pass? In the accomplishment of every vision, all these six points or characteristics must be seen or satisfied just as it was in the scenario in Genesis 11.
- The who: Come let us – all of them of one language [vss.3&4]

- The what: let us build a city [vs. 4]
- The way & how: they had brick for stone and slime for mortar [vs. 3]
- The why: for a reason - we will not be scattered abroad [vs. 4]
- The when: let us build now [vs. 4]
- The where: a plain in the land of Shinar where they dwelt [vs. 2]

7. Ministry begins with an assurance of your general, specific, personal and ministry covenant with God. When you understand the covenant you have, you have confidence and boldness to summon your covenant to deal with demons and hindrances that stand in the way of the fulfilment of your divine assignment. If you are sent, you must know the covenant that comes with your sending. Moses knew 'I am that I am' was with him to back up his words. So did David in 1 Samuel 17 – that's why he called Goliath an uncircumcised philistine. The apostles knew He would confirm the words they preached with signs and wonders. Jesus knowing He was sent by God was bold enough to say, 'the works I see him do is what I do also', etc.

8. Ministry requires addiction to hearing and obeying God's voice daily. Get into God's agenda daily.

9. Ministry originates with the spiritual before the physical. Ministry markets, products and customers are all spiritual. As a result, every approach to ministry must first be spiritual before anything else. Failure to understand and act accordingly will lead to unending frustration culminating in failure. - 1 Thessalonians 2:4-8
- Church growth is first spiritual, ministry is first spiritual. When a bill arises, the first thing you do must be to discern

spiritually as to whether this bill has arisen because of something I wanted or it was divinely authorized. (Lamentations 3:37) If it was of the flesh then I must find a way of paying for it or repent but if it was sanctioned from heaven, then I can call on heavenly supply – 'God I have done this at your instruction so I am expecting divine provision to meet this need; thank you for it in Jesus' name. Amen!' (Luke 22:35) In Acts 13, they preached the word of God, and God emptied the cities into the church. **PRAYER: LORD, EMPTY OUR CITIES INTO OUR CHURCHES IN JESUS' NAME!**

10. Ministry is only effective and sustainable when the rule of focus is consistently applied. If the enemy can steal your focus, he has your victory and testimony. You need to ask yourself, 'Why am I called and for what purpose?' - Matthew 6:22

a. SEE! Your cutting edge is your ability to be precise in what God has called you to do.
b. Leadership is lonely because of focus and people do not see the position as you (e.g. Elijah on Mount Carmel).
c. The enemy will do anything and everything to break your focus on the assignment God has committed to your hands.
d. The battle for exploits is won when you refuse to break your focus. ADVICE: Do not be diverted by running around solving diversion problems. Your prayer must be: 'Lord, keep my eyes single.'
e. Focus is the discipline and ability to concentrate and produce results when the circumstances are not right. Despite no friends, no money, no comfort, in ridicule, you are focussed like Paul in Romans 8:35-39.
f. If you are not focused in the ministry, you cannot last. For example: - **i.** SAMSON: When the Philistines caught Samson, even though his strength was in his hair, they

removed his eyes (vision). Without your eyes (sight/vision) you will be led to do what others want you to do. If your eyes are intact, if your eyes are full of light, then your whole body will be full of light. The person he was close to whose soul was knit to him caused him to lose focus. That's why Samson asked for vengeance for his eyes - his last prayer was, 'revenge my eyes.' (Judges 16:28) Disassociate from distracters - 1 Corinthians 15:33.
ii. DAVID: David's greatest error was committed when his focus was lost - 2 Samuel 11:1-4.
- It was at the time of least focus.
- The advice is: Don't lose your focus. Seek God's face first on everything.

g. If you sit in your office and you cannot see or hear, you are bound.

11. Ministry is not a relegation to a life of struggles and suffering but a fulfilled life. (John 10:10) So, get your instructions before stepping out.

12. Ministry is not a business or industry, but about people's destinies so do not treat it like one. The money changers were trying to help make the temple worship easier but displeased God; they were kicked out, because they made kingdom business a trade. - 2 Timothy 4:2

13. Ministry is not a journey of trial and error. It's not guess work.

14. Ministry begins with a definite calling because ministry requires a definite and particular call. With this definite call comes grace, abilities, provision, endowments, confidence, boldness, manpower, resources, accuracy and precision in activating spiritual gifts, guidance, protection, financial

provision, God's presence, weight, power and authority backing the words you speak and utter, confirmed with signs and wonders, angelic ministry, effectiveness, success and undeniable results / proofs.

a. With this in mind: It is a self-inflicted curse to embark on ministry out of circumstances, money needs, pride, strife, what you see others doing or the compliments or recommendations of people, etc. - Hebrews 5:4

b. Embarking on Ministry without a clear call is equivalent to a self-inflicted curse. I repeat: It is a self-inflicted curse to embark on any ministry enterprise that God did not call you to embark on. God will only finance what He commands you to embark on. In the kingdom, common sense is nonsense. Examples of those who only embarked on God's clear instructions and assignment which culminated in their provision being guaranteed are: Elijah (1 Kings 17); Elisha (2 Kings 4); Abraham (Genesis 12&22); Isaac (Genesis 26); Job (Job 22:17-28; 42); Noah (Gen. 6-8)

15. Ministry is: Knowing and being persuaded of if you are called, why you are called, who you are called to, where you are called, to whom you are called, when to step out, what you are called to do and say, staying where you are called and knowing how to accomplish your calling. BE AND GO WHERE HE TOLD YOU TO BE/GO, DO ONLY WHAT HE TOLD YOU TO DO AND STAY WHERE HE TOLD YOU TO STAY.

16. Ministry is what you are within you not what is on the outside. It is the transaction of covenant.

17. Ministry is not a popularity contest.

18. Ministry is not initially about you being famous but making Him known and famous and in the process of you exalting, lifting, glorifying Him and making Him known, you also become known because of Him. As confirmed in the following passage: John 12:32, 'And I, if I be lifted up from the earth, will draw all men unto me.'

19. The foundation for a successful ministry is not your eloquence – it is emphatically your divine calling.

20. Ministry begins with and is sustained by a heavenly calling. **In ministry there is no such thing as luck. If you are not heavenly-called, you have no heavenly backing and if you don't have heavenly backing, you are an easy target exposed to the gates of hell prevailing against you and even angels cannot help you.**

21. Ministry requires daily consultation with your Caller for clear, divine instructions that secure undisputed, maximum and lasting supernatural results. Your creativeness/creativity and innovation in ministry must be accompanied by and subjected to daily consultation with the Holy Spirit [the owner of the Church] for approval and divine direction.

- **In every endeavour of ministry, learn to submit your creativity to Divinity for instruction, approval, empowerment, correction or adjustment**. WHEN DIVINITY COMES UPON HUMANITY, IT RELEASES AN UNCOMMON PERSONALITY!

- If there is no call, there is no grace. (Ephesians 4:7)

- With this call comes a principle: Ministry begins with and is sustained by receiving four major instructions. You must of necessity receive these from God before you embark on your journey/enterprise in ministry:

They are namely:
a. Description
b. Inscription
c. Prescription and
d. Subscription.

- The statement: WRITE THE VISION DOWN in Habakkuk 2 means:
- **Describe it**
- **Inscribe it**
- **Prescribe For it and**
- **Subscribe To it.**

- 1st of all **describe it – define clearly what the vision is**.

- 2nd, **inscribe it – write it down so you don't keep changing it because of circumstances or people; also**, so it cannot be erased.

- 3rd, you must **take a prescription from God as to the How**! God said you will pastor a church of 10,000 - you have the target. Now, **wait on Him to tell you how. This is what you need to do so what I said will come to pass.** For you to be what you should be, take this prescription twice or thrice daily, hold this or that specialised or general relevant event daily, weekly, monthly or yearly.

- 4th, **subscribe to it** - after you've received the steps and prescription, **act upon it; do it; subscribe to the prescription. This ensures you don't sway from the original path.**

22. Ministry is not for personal gain but essentially and initially for the benefit of those you are assigned to serve and influence positively to influence others.

23. Ministry is about serving the people and not yourself. 'SERVING SELF MAKES A SLAVE, SERVING OTHERS MAKES A LEADER AND COMMITMENT TO SERVING OTHERS MAKES A GREAT LEADER.' - BISHOP OYEDEPO

24. Ministry is a yoke that is easy, not burdensome. If you are not called, ministry will be full of constant struggles and even suicidal tendencies.

Matthew 11:28-30, 'Come unto me, all ye that labour and are heavy laden, and I will give you rest. Take my yoke upon you, and learn of me; for I am meek and lowly in heart: and ye shall find rest unto your souls. For my yoke is easy, and my burden is light.'

1 Thessalonians 5:24, 'Faithful is he that calleth you, who also will do it.'

- If He called you, **He will do it, but if He did not call you then you will do it.**

25. Ministry is a tongue baptized with fire [not noise]. - Isaiah 6:6-8

26. Ministry is about being a news-maker not a noise-maker.

27. Ministry begins with a certified sending. People who are sent by God triumph divinely. 2 Corinthians 2:14, 'Now thanks be unto God, which always causeth us to triumph in

Christ, and maketh manifest the savour of his knowledge by us in every place.'

28. Ministry is not a career you decide upon; it is a divine calling: this knowledge will preserve you from pride and prevent you from leaping into endeavours which God did not commission. (1 Timothy 1:12)

a. Divine appointments avert severe disappointments. (Lam. 3:37)

b. Divinely-sent people triumph by God's hand. (2 Corinthians 2:14) Some say, 'Someone else has done it so I can also do it.' (Ephesians 4:7, 11) That kind of approach can floor you. Do you have the grace to do the same? NOTE: Venturing into someone's assignment can kill you.

29. Ministry is not fame, wealth, popularity, respect, position, radio or TV, Real Estate, your bank balance or the number of people in your church or ministry or being seen or heard of or known. (Acts 2:22-37; 2 Samuel 18:22-30)

30. Ministry requires diligence. Laziness is a guarantee for failure or stagnation in ministry. God does not put his seal of approval on lazy people. Laziness is not permitted in ministry.
a. Diligence and enterprising work pleases God. (2 Timothy 2:15; Hebrews 11:6; Proverbs 22:29; Ecclesiastes 5:3, 18-20; 3:13,22)
b. Laziness is not excessive sleep; it is missing opportunities such as failing to exercise yourself in your calling; am I productive with my time?
c. You will know if you are productive with your time if you are doing the following: Reading, studying and praying

more, engaged in more creative thinking, writing more books, manuals, training and raising leaders, etc.
d. Spiritual labour commands material blessings. (1 Timothy 5:17)
e. Labour to be filled with knowledge and increase your success potential.
f. Also engage yourself in self-development and personal development involving home-acquired knowledge to make you a more productive and better person.
g. Study and pray consistently during the week long before Sunday services or meetings.
h. Duplicate yourself in your protégés; mentoring does not have to be from the pulpit always – it can be on a one-on-one basis or in small groups.
i. Be Diligent in ministry because God sees our labour in secret and rewards us openly. God is not a debtor to anyone; if you spend faith, He will pay you back. When you sow a seed, He will pay you back before you ask for pay.
j. Engage in Spiritual Labours – Labours of insight, word and prayer, because our investment determines what God does for us; i.e. your input determines your output – what you sow determines what you reap. (Genesis 8:22)

REMEMBER:
- **Making the most of your time is making the most of your life, career and ministry. - 1 Thessalonians 4:11**
- **Wasting the most of your time is wasting the most of your life, career and ministry.**

31. Ministry is not just confession of faith but profession of your faith.

32. Ministry is your ability to know and understand the mind

of God and to communicate it effectively to people - saved or unsaved. If you don't know what God is saying [the heart of God] you are not in ministry - period! I need to know, 'What is the mind of God in different ways for our ministry - House of Judah? REASON BEING: I must communicate the heart of God.' We must be an oracle of God – the mouth-piece of God.
- **True ministers are oracles of the mind of God. (**2 Samuel 18**)**

33. Ministry is digging into the heart of God to reach men. It's downloading God's mind and heart to people. - Jeremiah 3:15

34. Ministry is preaching and teaching His message, [not yours or a good sermon]. (Ezekiel 2:4)
a. Anywhere you go to minister, place a demand on the Godhead, i.e. expect God to confirm what HE IS SAYING. Tremble at the concept of saying what He did not say or is not saying and putting a burden on people He did not put on them. THE VOICE OF GOD IS MIGHTY, VALUABLE AND PRECIOUS.

35. Ministry is OPERATING BY THE SENT WORD - go preach saying the kingdom of God is at hand…

EVERY TIME A SENT MAN SPEAKS, THE SENDER SHOWS UP to confirm what He has sent him to speak.

- John the Baptist came with a message of repentance. Jesus came initially with a message to the household of Israel.

36. Ministry is running and preaching His message, not your message.

37. Ministry is not cheap talk - it is hard, smart, creative work, backed by prayer, studying God's word, warfare, power, training and raising leaders but you should not struggle, toil or sweat. If ministry is a struggle, then revisit your calling because God promises us in Proverbs 4:18, that the path of the just is as the shining light that shineth more and more unto a perfect day. If you are fighting the same fight always, check it.

38. Ministry is not about the glory we see but settling down to investigate and understand the story behind what brings the glory.

39. Ministry is secured by heavenly backing. It is your calling into ministry that secures and guarantees heavenly backing. Is your church on God's agenda? Then He will supply every need. If God did not send you on TV then don't be there. Be in God's agenda or you will struggle.

40. Ministry is: Knowing and down-loading the mind of God [a specific message] to humanity - saved or unsaved. This implies that we musn't run without getting the message or else we'll be asked to stand aside like Ahimaaz.

- When you are asked, 'What message do you have for us?' like Ahimaaz whilst others like the Cushite who waited for the message will be asked to speak because they carried a message and had the mandate, you may be asked to stand aside. 2 Samuel 18:28-33, 'And Ahimaaz called, and said unto the king, All is well. And he fell down to the earth upon his face before the king, and said, Blessed be the LORD thy God, which hath delivered up the men that lifted up their hand against my lord the king. And the king said, Is the young man Absalom safe? And Ahimaaz answered, When Joab sent the king's servant, and me thy servant, I saw a great tumult, but I knew not what it was. And the king said unto him, Turn aside, and stand here. And he turned aside, and stood still. And, behold, Cushi came; and Cushi said, Tidings, my lord the king: for the LORD hath avenged thee this day of all them that rose up against thee. And the king said unto Cushi, Is the young man Absalom safe? And Cushi answered, The enemies of my lord the king, and all that rise against thee to do thee hurt, be as that young man is. And the king was much moved, and went up to the chamber over the gate, and wept: and as he went, thus he said, O my son Absalom, my son, my son Absalom! would God I had died for thee, O Absalom, my son, my son!'

So, wait for the message before moving.

41. Ministry is vision and mission – Joel 2. Your life must be driven by a God-ordained vision and mission. Don't mistake ambition for vision. **Vision is what God wants whilst ambition is what you want.**

42. Ministry - Church growth is a downloaded answer – it is downloaded from heaven. It is about what you heard.

43. Ministry is the things you do that are productive with value-adding traits [VAT]. It's about influencing your world positively by adding value to people, places, societies, communities and nations.

44. Ministry is hearing God and doing what God says. Before you do or say anything, make sure it is God you heard and are hearing.

45. Ministry is doing your job (and it will show) and doing

your job is knowing the mind of God. - John 5:39

46. Ministry is hearing, doing and delivering what is on God's heart, not what's on your mind. David was described as a man after God's own heart – a man that carried God's heart, a man that knew His heart. **WHAT WE SHOULD PURSUE IS THE MIND [heart] OF GOD AND THE THINGS WILL PURSUE US (Matthew 6:33).**

Knowing the mind of God is the biggest challenge and asset of a minister.

Scripture says in Proverbs 3:5-8 that we should trust in the Lord and lean not on our own understanding. (Don't go into that pulpit with your own mind but His mind and say what HE IS SAYING, SO HE CAN BACK IT UP!) In all our ways we should acknowledge Him that He would direct our paths.

Mark 16:15-20 says He went with them confirming the words they preached with signs following. If it's His word, He is obligated to and will confirm it with transformation of lives and signs and wonders but if it is your word then you will have to back it up with carnal strategies. The value and quality of your individual calling [material supply and provision] resides in the quality and value of your hearing God.
- DESIRE DRIVES YOUR ABILITY TO HEAR.
- Your wages for bearing the mind of God is paid by the One who sent you. (1 Kings 17; Luke 22:35)
- The people you are sent to are not your employers or employees. He said to the disciples, 'When I sent you did you lack anything? They said nothing.' (Luke 22:35)

REMEMBER: YOU ARE SENT TO THE PEOPLE NOT BY THE PEOPLE.

47. Ministry is a long distance haul not a hundred meter dash. Do not be frustrated with limited growth; rather enjoy the journey / process. - Exodus 23:28-30

48. Ministry is about accomplishments not entitlements for there is no entitlement in titles but in achievements.

49. Ministry begins with a CERTIFIED / DEFINITE SENDING.
a. **EVERY TIME A SENT MAN SPEAKS, THE SENDER [the one who sent him] SHOWS UP. So,** ministry must first of all begin with a certified sending and with that sending comes definite heavenly backing. Paul said he was not disobedient to the heavenly vision. Acts 26:19, 'Whereupon, O king Agrippa, I was not disobedient unto the heavenly vision:'
b. If heaven sent you then expect heavenly funding – funding from above through human vessels and angelic activations – heaven will speak to men and men will respond as they did for Elijah, Elisha, Jesus, Paul, etc.

50. Ministry has ranking and ranking is not the same thing as titles. Ranking is placement and sequence for collective good.
a. This army did not break its ranks: Joel 2:7, 'They shall run like mighty men; they shall climb the wall like men of war; and they shall march everyone on his ways, and they shall not break their ranks:'
b. Mark 6:40, 'And they sat down in ranks, by hundreds, and by fifties.'
c. **The Holy Spirit moves mightily where there is purpose, order, honour, keeping of ranks, oneness, unity, love and one accord.**
d. Joshua 9:2, 'That they gathered themselves together, to

fight with Joshua and with Israel, with one accord.'
e. Acts 2:46, 'And they, continuing daily with one accord in the temple, and breaking bread from house to house, did eat their meat with gladness and singleness of heart,'
f. Titus 1:5, 'For this cause left I thee in Crete, that thou shouldest set in order the things that are wanting, and ordain elders in every city, as I had appointed thee:'

51. Ministry is about accomplishments, not titles.

52. Ministry is about serving and adding value to others.

53. Ministry is solely about transforming, translating and transfiguring destinies.

54. Ministry involves an understanding of and eradication of certain diseases in churches. (Refer to page 98 of PASTORAL LEADERSHIP 101)

55. Ministry is a journey not a brief trip.

56. Ministry involves challenges and solving problems - it is not void of problems. With greatness in ministry comes a perpetuation of tests, trials, problems and challenges. It comes with the terrain – new heights, new levels and new devils to deal with. So have and show mercy (by applying oil and wine) for the sheep; but 'a rod and fight' for the wolf when it shows up in the house. Psalm 34:19 says, 'Many are the afflictions of the righteous: but the LORD delivereth him out of them all.' (John 16:33; 2 Corinthians 4:17-18)

57. Ministry is full of all kinds of opposition. There are two kinds of opposition in ministry [Spiritual and physical]. Expect to have to deal with both kinds from time to time (and

remember that it is a normal process of ministry).

58. Ministry is about impact. Until your ministry has an impact on the outside world you've not started ministry.

59. Ministry is sustained by an understanding of and operating in both your personal and ministry covenants [General, Specific, Personal and Ministry Covenants].

60. Ministry involves an understanding of and activation of Angelic Ministry [How to deploy angels to work for you, those you are called to and your entire ministry]. (Hebrews 1:14; Psalm 103:20)

61. Ministry is about pouring into, empowering, developing and raising men; not raising offerings or money. After you raise men, empower them and develop them to fulfil destiny, there will be more than enough money to do what you are called to do. REMEMBER: **Money does not make ministry - it is ministry that makes money.**

62. Ministry involves preaching (pandering and responding) to what's in your spirit, not what you see. Provide depth for your spirit and message. If you tailor your message for the people, they are leading you (and the ministry). Jeremiah 1 - What you see in your spirit is what is performed.

63. Lasting ministry requires solid sustainable structures both for now and the future. Church growth is sustainable. To achieve sustainability of continuous acceleration and impact we must put structures in place for our destination and also what we preach must be structured. Preaching must not be done just anyhow - one subject must be taught at a time and dealt with in detail for clear understanding and application of

the subject matter resulting in daily proofs in the lives of the flock i.e. What is taught must be clearly understood, practised and become lifestyle, for e.g. faith, finance, praise, outreach, dominion, faithfulness, loyalty, etc.

64. Disappointment in ministry is eradicated with divine appointment. You cannot be disappointed in ministry if you are appointed by God. I was appointed by God to do what I am doing. It is He who is working in me both to will and to do of His own good pleasure. There is no room for pride when I know He is the One working in me. – Lamentations 3:37, 'Who is he that saith, and it cometh to pass, when the Lord commandeth it not?'

65. Ministry involves being on the lookout for opportunities to maximize your potential and opportunities.

66. Ministry must begin with an understanding of the know-how - it takes wisdom to sustain a divine move. Principles backed by power will guarantee the future outcome of any church or ministry. A minister shouldn't embark upon a journey that will cost him/her everything (burning the bridges behind them - like Elisha did with his family) if they do not know the sure route to the destination – the how. (Proverbs 4:7)

67. Sustained Ministry requires all that you are and all that you own. It takes everything you are and have to do something significant for God. Jesus said get a **CROSS,** not a **CROWN**. The Cross produces the Crown.

68. Every marvellous, mighty experience or achievement in ministry is definitely an act of God. Psalm 118:23 says, 'This is the LORD'S doing; it is marvellous in our eyes.' And Psalm

78:12 reads: 'Marvellous things did he in the sight of their fathers, in the land of Egypt, in the field of Zoan.'

69. Sustained ministry requires adequate relevant ongoing preparation. When God is going to do something, prepare in the draught (and not when the rain comes pouring down.) Because, the blessing [rain] will drown the unprepared. - 1 Kings 18:41-45; Hebrews 10:36-38
- Noah could not build the ark in the flood.
- Ahab could not run in the storm (that's why fore-warning was given in each instance).

70. Ministry requires and involves being delivered from the people. Acts 26:17, 'Delivering thee from the people, and from the Gentiles, unto whom now I send thee,'

71. Ministry requires excellence not mediocrity. If you are not prepared to set your sights on 'awesome' (unction and glory) then quit ministry. **Mediocrity is not the language of the ministry. EXCELLENCE IS!**

72. **Impactful and life-transforming ministry is initiated, not waited for. The next move of God in your life is entirely up to you. Discard the doctrine of waiting for God; God is waiting for you to 'pay the price – the required price.'**

73. Productive ministry requires cognisance of the promises more than the challenges. Know and be acquainted with the PROMISES of God to you and your ministry. Otherwise you will not know what to expect or how to prepare for it (or recognise it when it comes.)

The PROMISE must be more real to you than the PROBLEM. Starve the problems by paying them no attention; feed the promises instead.

74. Ministry requires a deliberate pacing of oneself for the journey. Take time out periodically to push back the chair and evaluate. Do not run yourself down spiritually, emotionally, psychologically or physically.

75. Ministry demands a covenant attitude of gratitude each step of the way. Thank God for where you are to activate God's hand for the next level. As you express gratitude for where you are and what you have, you commit God to take you to the next level. (Exodus 23:28-30) **Thankful people always have their tanks full**.

76. Ministry which originated as a divine mandate cannot be achieved by fleshly methods/effort or in the energy of the flesh. A heavenly calling therefore requires the question, 'What am I divinely mandated to do?'

77. Ministry is walking according to the will of God. Don't step into anything until you know for sure, that is the will of God for you: **Being set apart for the Master's use.**

Proverbs 4:18 says, 'The path of the just is as the shining light, that shineth more and more unto the perfect day.'

From Genesis 1, we discover: **God creates, God moves and God speaks and so does the Church. The church creates, the church moves and the church speaks.**

If you can see it, you can have it. The quality of decisions we make is governed by the degree of information we have.

78. Sustained ministry requires praying without ceasing - strategic, spiritual warfare and all manner of prayer. (Ephesians 6; James 5:17-18)

i. Prayer eases the birthing of vision; informed prayer.
ii. It urges a manifestation of internal vision and foresight.
iii. We must have a greater understanding of prayer.
iv. Pray the promise, not the problem.
v. Prayer that is not praying the promise is ineffective prayer – pray the promise not the problem.
vi. Pray the promise. When we pray the promise we are boasting in God.
vii. Praying the promise activates angels on our behalf.

79. Ministry presents challenges and problems that must be solved.
- A Minister must develop a good attitude towards challenges/problems.
- Problems are normal in ministry terrain.
- Problems come in different shapes and sizes – in the form of people, things, issues, challenges, etc.

80. Timing is everything in ministry.
i. Never be in a hurry to acquire or achieve what heaven has not sanctioned. (Proverbs 28:22)
ii. Do not eat dinner too soon (in the morning). (Ecclesiastes 10:16-17)
- Anything you get too fast will definitely not last. [It leaves just as fast]
- Bid your time and allow the process to take its full course.
- Haste is hazardous.
iii. When greatness comes, it often does not come in the form you were expecting it. Often it is a hand in the sky or seed and not a forest. (e.g. Elijah's storm was first a little hand)

81. Effective Ministry will require all that you have and all that you are.

82. Success in ministry is the implementation of set goals and tasks, such as a target of 10 to start, 20 by end, etc.

83. Success in ministry can be defined in the face of a clear assignment or purpose. Paul said, 'I strive for the mark of the high calling in Christ Jesus.' If there is no mark, you are striving in the wrong direction.

84. Success in ministry is not measured by comparison with others but with set goals such as how many of the set goals were achieved.

85. Greatness in ministry requires being controversial sometimes and criticized. REMEMBER: Greatness, criticism and controversial often go hand in hand. Do not be afraid of being controversial in the pursuit of greatness. The enemy's comments are irrelevant.
a. There will be times when you will be at odds with those who serve you. They will from time to time not see what you see (or hear what you hear). [Such as: Elijah saying, 'I hear the sound of an abundance of rain;' or Elisha saying to Gehazi, '…….those with us are more than those against us;' or Joshua instructing 'let's walk round the walls of Jericho' or Moses stretching his rod in response to 'go forward into the Red Sea…'
b. God said to Abraham, 'I will make your name great'; (not title)
    - **Greatness is intrinsic and not contagious.**
    - **Greatness is released in steps and stages.**
c. Do not scuffle with those you are sent to teach. Servants/sons should be taught and trained to submit and be obedient without necessarily seeing or understanding it. The power of mantle/anointing transference is in seeing what I see. 'If you see what I see when I am taken from you.' (Elijah, Elisha).

d. Do not be fooled by what people SAY; be cautious to consider what people DO more importantly.

86. Ministry requires diligence, discipline, determination and sacrifice. There are rules and there are regulations to fulfilling ministry and remember it is hard work.

87. In ministry there is no such thing as luck. Fools believe in luck whilst the wise believe in the principle or law of cause and effect.

88. If you are not called, ministry will be full of constant struggles. 1 Thessalonians 5:24 says, 'Faithful is he that calleth you, who also will do it.' If He called you, He will do it, but if He did not call you then you will do it or bring it to pass through carnal strategies.

89. Ministry is not fulfilled by intentions but by required actions. You don't sleep with vision - you run with vision just like prophecies don't fulfil themselves but prophecies are fulfilled through pursuit of purpose, focus, sacrifice, effective use and management of time, dogged determination, discipline, devotion, continuous learning, acquisition and application of the required skill, an addiction to excellence, being under an effective proven mentor, contention in warfare [battle] and hard smart creative work within purpose. That is why a Leading ministry is usually a need-meeting ministry.

90. In ministry, God is only committed to what He commands. For example in Judges 6:14, 'And the LORD looked upon him, and said, Go in this thy might, and thou shalt save Israel from the hand of the Midianites: have not I sent thee?'

91. Ministry is not for Novices.

92. Ministry requires the right attitude – you attitude determines your altitude.

93. Guaranteed Provision for ministry begins with a certified call and sending. God pays for what He sends as indicated in Luke 22:35.

94. Ministry is not about pursuit of money or making money at the expense of others. It's about impact. 'MONEY DOESN'T MAKE MINISTRY - IT IS MINISTRY THAT MAKES MONEY.' - BISHOP OYEDEPO

95. Ministry is not about raising offerings but raising men.

96. Ministry requires a complete knowledge and understanding of what He said and is saying.

97. Ministry is not equal to ambition. Scripture says in Hebrews 5:4, 'And no man taketh this honour unto himself, but he that is called of God, as was Aaron.'

REMEMBER that In Ministry:
- One must never mistake ambition for vision.
- Ambition leads to frustration.
- Ambition has fatalistic outcome - it brings or is a cancer to ministry.
- Ambition says 'me' whilst calling says 'Him'. The proof that God sent you is in the supernatural results. Ambition is a desire to be seen.
- Unfortunately, many mistake ambition for vision. Divine calling says God said and He will do it. Ambition says me and I will do it. **Vision is what God wants whilst ambition is what you want.**

98. Ministry is embracing a divine agenda, not a personal or man-made agenda or ambition. With every suggestion and idea, ask yourself, 'Is this part of His divine agenda/mandate for me or not?' REASON: You will squander a move when you embrace a non-divine agenda.

99. Ministry is not just about going to collect a loan, hire a hall, fill it with chairs and musical instruments and see if people will come. No! It begins with a definite calling, preparation, equipment, sending, backing from the Sender, staying in touch with the Sender and operating as commanded.

100. Ministry requires all you are and all that you have and keeping your eyes single by sitting on your assignment. 'DON'T SUCCEED OUTSIDE AND FAIL AT HOME.' - ARCHBISHOP BENSON IDAHOSA

101. Ministry requires paying the required price. - DON'T MAKE THE MISTAKE OF KEEPING YOUR EYES ON THE GLORY OF MINISTRY WITHOUT SETTLING DOWN TO UNDERSTAND THE STORY BEHIND THE GLORY.

102. Ministry will inflict scars on you and in you so, stay resolute. Success both in life and ministry is not only measured by what a man achieves/accomplishes, but by the opposition he has encountered, and the courage/fortitude with which he has maintained the struggle against overwhelming odds. REMEMBER: The measure of a man is the way he bears up under misfortune. IN MINISTRY PEOPLE WILL EITHER BE AN ASSET TO YOU OR A LIABILITY. BE COURAGEOUS AND FOCUSSED!

103. Effective ministry requires a persuasion of what you are equipped and empowered to accomplish. You are not

equipped to do everything.
- Every church and Pastor has an emphasis.
- What is your emphasis?
- What is the vision, the mandate, the agenda of your ministry?
- You must have a revelation of what you are called to do.
- When they wake you up from bed, what springs out of you automatically?
- What is your core message?
- Ezekiel said, 'I prophesied as I was commanded.'
- What have you been commanded to prophesy and to who?
- You should know where you are sent. You don't go just anywhere. Jonah liked Tarshish but he was sent to Nineveh. The fact that you are an African and are from Africa does not necessarily mean you may be sent to Africa or called to Africans, e.g. David Livingstone, a white man was called to Africa, Reinhard Bonkke, a white man to Africa, Sunday Adelaja, a black man to Ukraine, etc.
- Your calling has a 'what', a 'where', a 'when', a 'who', a 'with whom', a 'when', a 'why', a 'which' and a 'way' or 'how'.
- Be careful how you apply them. It is not everything that is now. When you have and are preaching the sent word and your voice is blessed from heaven, people will hear you and want to hear you any day; they never get bored or tired of hearing you and they will look for you – they will come and find you. You will be a sought-out one – Isaiah 55 & 62.

104. Ministry involves reformation and transformation. We are men on a mission to produce effective global spiritual, physical, economic, mental, transformation, translation, transfiguration and social reformation in every sphere of life. We are here to turn the world upside down with the right side up. Acts 17:6 says, 'And when they found them not, they drew Jason and certain brethren unto the rulers of the city,

crying, These that have turned the world upside down are come hither also;'
- **Revival is not what goes on in your building. Until your ministry has an impact on the outside world, you've not started ministry.**

105. Ministry requires as of necessity daily communion with God for fresh manna and instruction.

106. Effective ministry requires full dedication.

107. Ministry is vision and mission – accomplishing a divine mission /mandate (Joel 2:7). Ministry is an army that does not break its ranks. Ministry has ranking and ranking is not the same thing as titles. Ranking is placement and sequence for collective good. Where they were placed, they stayed there. There will be different churches - all significant. Don't form your church according to another's pattern. God will reward us for faithfulness to what He has called us to do, not according to size. Understand the vision of God for your church. Be yourself, not someone else. Don't copy people's calling; you have your own calling.

- 2 Corinthians 10:12 says, 'For we dare not make ourselves of the number, or compare ourselves with some that commend themselves: but they measuring themselves by themselves, and comparing themselves among themselves, are not wise.' Come to God and ask him to tell you what to do. Whatever you do, don't copy someone's assignment.

108. Ministry is not a career or venture you embark on or about personal ambition or popularity but about fulfilling destiny which calls for great sacrifice for your assignment backed by focus, discipline, determination, diligence and dedication.

'To win without risk is to triumph without glory.' [From frontline leadership mini-book by Dr. Myles Munroe]

109. Effective ministry requires a zero tolerance for procrastination, time-stealers and time-wasters. The time is short. Make every day and every minute count now and for eternity. Be careful about the passage of time. Anything left to time stays the same. Procrastination is a deadly weapon of the enemy '…a little sleep, a little slumber, a little more sleep…. and poverty will come on you as an armed robber.' (Proverbs 6:10-11) Poverty is a lack of productivity, so, utilise your time well. Don't allow time-wasters around you. If people don't respect your time, they don't respect you or your gift. Make daily decisions that have eternal value and consequences. [Get my book the Dangers of Procrastination)

110. Ministry is about setting yourself on fire and people coming to watch you burn and catching your consistent fire to go set others on fire for Christ, kingdom purposes and to pursue their assignments in life.

111. Lasting ministry is not built on bringing in guest speakers always – train the flock to know and heed your voice – Jesus said, 'My sheep know my voice.' - STOP INVITING GUEST SPEAKERS ON AN ONGOING BASIS TO MILK, HARASS AND ERAZE YOUR MEMBERS BY RAISING AND RAISING OFFERINGS THROUGH CARNAL, MARKETING AND PUBLIC RELATIONS STRATEGIES. YOU DON'T BUILD A LASTING MONUMENTAL CHURCH ON GUEST SPEAKERS.

112. Ministry is about impacting your world, your generation within and without the four walls of the church and beyond [with posterity clearly in mind]. Revival and causing waves is

not what goes on in your building only. Until your ministry has an impact outside the four walls of your church that cannot be erased, you've not entered or started ministry.

113. Ministry is fulfilled according to His pattern. You are destined for upward movement only if you will conduct ministry His way–**according to the pattern** shown you. Hebrews 8:5, 'Who serve unto the example and shadow of heavenly things, as Moses was admonished of God when he was about to make the tabernacle: for, See, saith he, that thou make all things according to the pattern showed to thee in the mount.'

114. Impactful and life-transforming ministry is initiated, not waited for. **The next move of God in your life is entirely up to you. Discard the doctrine of waiting for God; God is waiting for you to 'pay the price – the required price.'**

115. Ministry begins with and is sustained by an understanding of and a persuasive settlement of whether you are called into full-time ministry or part-time [helps and marketplace ministry] and staying with it.

116. Ministry must always begin with a certified and definite calling:

a. Without a calling, ministry is more or less like a curse because it will be devoid of divine backing because Jesus said, 'Without me ye can do nothing.' Embarking on any ministry-related enterprise without a calling is tantamount to unending struggles and heartaches.

b. So, ministry begins with an understanding of your calling either into pastoral or itinerant [travelling ministry].

117. Ministry begins, grows and expands essentially by understanding the following: The 'who', the 'why', the 'where', the 'whom', the 'which', the 'where', the 'what' and the 'how' [the way]. That makes the journey colourful and fulfilling.

118. Ministry is sustained by a vigorous no-nonsense pursuit of your purpose in life. Proverbs 27:8, 'As a bird that wandereth from her nest, so is a man that wandereth from his place.'

119. Ministry involves knowing, being persuaded of your originality, staying original and not compromising your originality by being a photocopy of someone else whilst catching the spirit and embracing the virtues / disciplines of your mentors/father in the Lord.

120. Ministry is not for weaklings but fighters – warriors.
- MINISTRY IS NOT FUNFARE; IT IS WARFARE!
- MINISTRY IS NOT A PLAYGROUND BUT A BATTLEGROUND!
- YOU DON'T SLEEP WITH VISION OR PROPHECY – YOU RUN, WAGE WAR, WORK AND WAR WITH IT!
- LIFE DOES NOT GIVE YOU WHAT YOU DESERVE BUT WHAT YOU DEMAND THROUGH CONTENTION IN BATTLE!
- BATTLES ARE WON ON THE PREMISE OF CONTENTION! - 'Rise ye up, take your journey, and pass over the river Arnon: behold, I have given into thine hand Sihon the Amorite, king of Heshbon, and his land: begin to possess it, and contend with him in battle.' (Deuteronomy 2:24)
For example, Daniel had to war with the prophecy concerning their return to their homeland from captivity. Recommended Reading: Read the book of Daniel chapter 10. **PROPHECIES**

DON'T FULFIL THEMSELVES NEITHER DO YOU SLEEP WITH VISION. They are warred into reality as instructed in 1 Timothy 1:18 –19 with emphasis on vs. 18, "This charge I commit unto thee son Timothy according to the prophecies which went before on thee, that thou by them mightest war a good warfare; Holding faith and a good conscience which some having put away concerning faith have made shipwreck;" (KJV)

AMPLIFIED VERSION says, "This charge and admonition I commit in trust to you, Timothy, my son, in accordance with prophetic intimations which I formerly received concerning you, so that inspired and aided by them you may wage the good warfare……."

That by them – that in their power or in the power of them [those prophetic words that have been spoken over your life/ministry] son, Timothy, use those words and war or wage a good warfare or inspired and aided by those prophetic words you may wage a good warfare.

121. REMEMBER: **The most important thing in ministry is to love God. Don't love your vision so much that you neglect God.**

122. In Ministry, Love is the key. (Matthew 22:35-39)
a. Love is the overriding and motivating force.
b. Love for God.
c. Love for Jesus.
d. Love for His people.
e. Love for His purpose.

123. The Ministry has everything to do with people.
a. It is called 'The People's Business'.

b. There is no future for any leader or ministry who is out to use people.
c. Serving others makes a leader - serving self makes a slave.

124. REMEMBER:
a. Ministry is about people, not you – **It's People-related Ministry.**
b. Raise men, not offerings/money and you'll have all you need.
c. Bless people with all your heart when you preach, teach or talk to them and minister to them; leave them blessed.
d. Your prayer must be, 'They must become better people. God show me something that will empower them to be better to walk in dominion.'
e. **Revelation comes to you when you have such a craving and desire for people to be blessed with truth.**
f. People will gather anywhere where the grass is green and remains green – Psalm 23.
g. Bless them from your heart and they'll come from everywhere to hear you.
h. Don't charge people or levy them financially; bless people.
i. Don't preach to impress people. Preach to bless and impact them. Neither you nor your ministry will ever lack if you give yourself for them.
j. Seek their welfare, not their stuff. Give your whole life to bless the people of God selflessly. 2 Corinthians 12:14 says, 'Behold, the third time I am ready to come to you; and I will not be burdensome to you: **for I seek not yours, but you**: for the children ought not to lay up for the parents, but the parents for the children.'
Paul said, 'I do not seek yours but you. I am not coming to ask for your stuff, but to seek your/their prosperity, success and progress.'
k. Stop going for your members' pockets. The Law of connection says, 'You touch a heart before you ask for

a hand.' As we discovered in my leadership manual: 'Pastoral Leadership 101' if you touch them, they will in turn touch you.

l. God does not need men or money to execute His intentions. (Psalm 50:7-15) He needs faith, [Hebrews 11:6] because without faith it is impossible to please [move] Him and when a man's ways please the LORD, he maketh even his enemies to be at peace with him. (Proverbs 16:7)

- Luke 22:35, 'And he said unto them, When I sent you without purse, and scrip, and shoes, lacked ye any thing? And they said, Nothing.'

The man by the pool said he did not have anyone to put him in the pool when the Word, Jesus was right by the pool. It begins by faith and men come and put it together. God has prepared a total stranger to come in and give towards that cause. Pastor, don't dream according to the paper computations. We must walk by faith and do exploits for the kingdom. You don't need partners to do the work of God – you need heavenly partnership.

125. Ministry requires heavenly approval and heavenly partnership. If you have heavenly approval and heavenly partnership, all you need to accomplish the mandate God has assigned to you, will be provided so you definitely accomplish it – it is made possible by heavenly backing.

126. Success in ministry is not measured by the quantity of accumulated possession, neither is it measured by popularity but rather consists of the attainment of God's goals and purposes for one's life as God told the prophet in Jeremiah 29:11. Discovering your God-given assignment and pursuing it is what ministry is.

127. My father in the Lord said: 'MINISTRY: Is neither a dream nor a trance. It's not a church title or leadership position held in a local Church. It's not an organisation or an association but rather a divine assignment handed down to a person by God. It is stewardship – serving as a messenger to carry out the orders of your superior. It is not an idea, a feeling or a burden but carrying out a given task. It is harnessing divine resources to carry out divine assignments committed into a man's hand. It is not limited to pulpit or to preaching as it were but covers every area of human need - social, moral, spiritual, physical, mental, etc. So, wherever divine intervention is needed for the gospel of the kingdom to be enhanced, God always dispatches human agents to stand in for Him and on his behalf.' (Amos 3:7; Isaiah 44:26)

128. The strength of your ministry and the guarantee of your supplies lie in the depth of your commitment to your core assignment. (Luke 8:1-3; 22:35) The strength of any ministry therefore is not in its spread, but in its depth; so preach the Word in season and out of season. (2 Timothy 4:2) Do not let anything or anyone take you off your core assignment because that is what determines your overall success in ministry.

129. Ministry essentially means a minister bearing a message that meets the needs of mankind through the instrumentality of the Word. (Acts 6)

130. Preaching the Word is what makes ministry and ministry is what makes money. The WORD is what determines the quality of your ministry which in turn determines the quality of life you enjoy.

131. Ministry is not just a commitment; it is a commission.

132. Ministry is a divine appointment not a self-appointment.

133. Ministry demands a definite and clearly-defined message – that is the core assignment of one's ministry.

134. Ministry is Word-made and Word-based. At the centre of every great ministry is the Word. (Acts 6:1-7; 2:37-47; 4:4, 30-32)

135. Ministry demands you look to God as your main Source. The day you start having human sponsors for your ministry is the day God stops being your sponsor. Human sponsors will pocket and limit your ministry. No matter the needs of your ministry, God has all it takes to meet them all. **Your resources are not in the hands of men but in His hands.**

136. A successful ministry is highly dependent on a successful family life.

137. Behind every successful ministry is a successful family life.

138. The Level of Opposition you face in ministry reveals your strong position.

139. The reality of an Open heaven over a ministry/church requires the Pastor to be a covenant practitioner – i.e. to be a tithing and giving Pastor and the ministry to remain a tithing and giving ministry/church.

140. Ministry is impossible without the anointing (Isaiah 11:1-3; Zechariah. 4:6-7)

2

17 FUNDAMENTAL LAWS FOR FULFILLING YOUR MINISTRY

Colossians 4:17, 'And say to Archippus, Take heed to the ministry which thou hast received in the Lord, that thou fulfil it.'

That you have received a ministry does not mean you will fulfil it. Take heed - get to know what you are called to do, what you must do and what it takes or what it requires and give it all it takes to fulfil the ministry you have received from the Lord. Remember, it must be a ministry you have received from the Lord that you fulfil, not a ministry you designed for yourself but a ministry delivered from the Lord - what He gave you. If the vision is not from the Lord you will be the one to fulfil it. Calling yourself into ministry is a self-inflicted curse. If it is Him, you position yourself, doing what He tells you to do and He steps in to fulfil it so we don't mistake ambition and impressions as vision. That you see a need does not mean God has called you to fulfil it - Are you the one sent to fulfil it? **A need is not equal to a calling on your life. That there is a need is not equal to a calling on your life. There are needs every day. An open door is not equal to an open vision.**

So fulfilling your vision begins with knowing it's from the Lord. If it is not from the Lord it will not be fulfilled. God said to the prophet in Jeremiah 27:15 says, 'For I have not sent them, saith the LORD, yet they prophesy a lie in my name; that I might drive you out, and that ye might perish, ye, and the prophets that prophesy unto you.'

In the above passage, God said of some, I have not sent these prophets yet they run; I have not sent them yet they prophesy. So, there are people running a race they have not been assigned like Ahimaaz in 2 Samuel 18. Psalm 32:9 says, 'Be ye not as the horse, or as the mule, which have no understanding: whose mouth must be held in with bit and bridle, lest they come near unto thee.'

Get your definite calling, definite instructions, specific message and specific location for its fulfilment from the Manufacturer before stepping out. The purpose for leadership and ministry is not the maintenance of followers but the production of more leaders/ministers/ministries so you must be equipped to do so. 2 Peter 1:10 says giving all diligence - give it all it requires. There are requirements you must meet to fulfil that ministry to make your calling sure. There are vital forces you must engage to fulfil your ministry. Ministry cannot fulfil itself no matter how good it appears. There are rules and there are regulations to fulfilling ministry and remember it is hard work. Hard work is the only way to become a high flier. Jesus said, 'I must work the works of him that sent me for the night cometh when no man can work.'

Ministry is not a calling into laziness; it is a calling into doing what is more than normal - Paul said in 1 Corinthians 15:10, 'I laboured more abundantly than them all.'

SO, NO LAZY MAN HAS A FUTURE IN MINISTRY.

There are fundamental laws that you must obey to fulfil your ministry. **Fulfilment is not so much about getting results; it's much more about getting results to match or meet the aspirations and the expectations of the Caller or Master [the One who called you]. So, it's important to stay spiritually awake. Unto whom much is given, much is required. He will require of you to the level that He has put in your hand.** So: Concentrate; put all your eggs in one basket, and watch that basket. As Liz Ashe said, "Don't try to be great at all things. Pick a few things to be good at and be the best you can." **Focus! Leaders are individuals who have declared independence from the expectations of others.**

So let's examine: The FUNDAMENTAL LAWS THAT WILL ENHANCE OR GUARANTEE FULFILMENT OF MINISTRY i.e. LAWS TO ENGAGE IN, IN FULFILLING YOUR MINISTRY i.e. the rules and regulations you must comply with which will help to add to the rate of the amazing results we are attracting. He said, 'my yoke is easy and my burden is light.' **If it is not easy it is not his yoke.** That you have a ministry doesn't mean you will fulfil it. Pursue it skilfully and intelligently. God is leaving you with the responsibility to fulfil it. Unto whom much is given, much is required. If God has assigned you to pastor a church of 2000 and you are pastoring a church of 1000 you have not fulfilled your ministry. Everyone might be clapping for you but much more than that is expected of you. We are to adapt to those rules and regulations that will enable us fulfil his mandate on our lives. There are rules, there are regulations that will help you arrive at your destination - if you don't mind them, then you are selling off your birthright. REMEMBER: **It takes a studious man to secure a glorious destiny. So,** 'Study to show thyself approved unto God, a workman that needeth not to be ashamed, rightly dividing the word of truth.' (2 Timothy 2:15)

- Only those who obey rules become rulers and only those who comply with laws become lords.

So, for you to fulfil your ministry indeed, you must enjoy the laws of scriptures. Every law of scriptures is a law of life. He has delivered us from the law of sin and death through the law of the operation of law of life in Christ Jesus.

Anchor Scripture: 2 Timothy 2:3-5, 'Thou therefore endure hardness, as a good soldier of Jesus Christ. No man that warreth entangleth himself with the affairs of this life; that he may please him who hath chosen him to be a soldier. And if a man also strive for masteries, yet is he not crowned, except he strive lawfully.'

Another translation says: 'No athlete wins the prize except he does it according to the rules - by applying himself to the rules of the game.'

Every calling into ministry requires everything that you are and everything that you have. **Ministry is fulfilled by abiding by the following laws some of which [*] originated from the teaching and book: EXPLOITS IN MINISTRY (A book I highly recommend) by my father in the Lord, Bishop David Oyedepo and my manuals - PASTORAL LEADERSHIP 101 and MINISTRY 101**: [You can order copies from www.dphstore.co.uk and from our website www.houseofjudah.org.uk].

I. The first is law is what I call the Law of DEFINITIVENESS OF PURPOSE: A discovery of your purpose and that of your ministry from God is crucial and non-negotiable in fulfilling your ministry and your destiny.

Why are you here? What is your ministry called to do? EVERYTHING STARTS WITH YOUR SOURCE and your PURPOSE. Proverbs 27:8, 'As a bird that wandereth from her nest, so is a man that wandereth from his place.'

- Definitiveness of purpose is the starting point of destiny, impact, fulfilment in life and all wealth.

IT IS SAID THAT: THE GREATEST TRAGEDY IN LIFE IS TO BE ALIVE AND NOT KNOW WHY YOU ARE ALIVE!

'As a bird that wandereth from her nest, so is a man that wandereth from his place [purpose/assignment].' To fulfil destiny, you must discover your assignment in life which empowers you to decide exactly what you want, write it down and then make a plan for its accomplishment. Leaders know that they possess the capacity to be leaders within the sphere of the purpose for which they were born. Discover and fulfil your ministry – don't wait; know and do your part. Mother Teresa put it this way: "I am a little pencil in the hand of a writing God, who is sending a love letter to the world." Singleness of purpose is one of the chief essentials for success in life, no matter what may be one's aim. As Kalvin Clause Witz said, "Pursue one great decisive aim with force and determination."

REMEMBER:
DESTINY IS NOT DECIDED; DESTINY IS DISCOVERED!

THE IMPORTANCE OF PURPOSE: (21 keys)
1. **Where purpose is unknown abuse is inevitable.**
2. Everything must begin with a purpose.
3. Where there is no bearing life becomes a burden.
4. Anyone who lacks bearing, purpose or direction in life becomes a burden on his family, on people, society and the nation. Proverbs 27:8, 'As a bird that wandereth from her nest, so is a man that wandereth from his place or purpose.'
5. The greatest tragedy in life is to be alive and not know why you are alive and the greatest form of waste is wasted potential due to a lack of discovery of your 'wiring' or why you are 'wired'/gifted the way you are.
6. Most people who are frustrated in life are those who have not as yet discovered their purpose or are not pursuing or fulfilling their purpose in life.
7. LIFE IS NOT MEASURED BY DURATION BUT BY

DONATION, i.e. contributions made for the benefit of others and society motivated by purpose.
8. Purpose gives you a reason for living and a drive to succeed in life.
9. Purpose is what gives one a reason for living, not one's job. 'For I know the thoughts that I think toward you, saith the LORD, thoughts of peace, and not of evil, to give you an expected end. – Jeremiah 29:11
10. YOU WILL ONLY FIND FULFILMENT IN YOUR GOD-GIVEN, GOD-ORDAINED/PREDESTINED PURPOSE. (Jeremiah 1:5-10)
11. Your purpose in life must be something you are ready to live and die for like Esther. (Esther 4:13-14)
12. When you discover your purpose, you don't settle for the status quo or negative statements of people around you or the dictates of the economy - you rise up and get violent at the expense of your life.
13. Without purpose life is just an existence.
14. When you discover your purpose, you are ready to die for it.
15. Your purpose is the reason for your life.
16. Your purpose is the reason for which God has given you a lease of life.
17. Those with no purpose did not show up here.
18. UNTIL YOU ARE READY TO DIE FOR SOMETHING, YOU ARE NOT READY TO LIVE FOR ANYTHING.
19. The greatest achievers in life are those who discovered the purpose for which they were willing to die.
20. Your PURPOSE IN LIFE IS WHAT MAKES LIFE MEANINGFUL. A discovery of your purpose in life gives you meaning, focus and fulfilment
21. When someone has a purpose for which they are ready to die and you have a purpose for which you are not ready to die, don't compete with him. When you have a purpose

you are not ready to die for, you back out at the slightest challenge and crisis or hard times. What are you here for? What meaning do you give to your own life? The value of life is not in how long a person lives alone, but in how that life was lived in pursuit and fulfilment of its God-given purpose.

II. The second law is the Law of DISCOVERIES:
- Discovery brings recovery.
- Discover your purpose, your strengths, your weaknesses, your potential – gifts and talents – what you do best with ease backed by proofs even without training and add skill, excellence and diligence for maximum productivity and discover opportunities in which to use them.
- Life is not fulfilled by intentions but by deliberate action.
- Anything left to chance does not stand a chance. Jeremiah started off by making discoveries about his purpose and 'wiring' by meeting with God to introduce him to himself and his assignment in life. Jeremiah 1:5, 'Before I formed thee in the belly I knew thee; and before thou camest forth out of the womb I sanctified thee, and I ordained thee a prophet unto the nations.'
- Get to know what you are here for before stepping out.
- Discover your potential – who you really are but no one has seen yet; what you are capable of becoming, doing and achieving but haven't become, done or achieved yet.
- You do this by meeting with and making discoveries from God who is your Source and your manufacturer and then adding skill and value to what I call your 'wiring' - your gifts and strengths to use it to add value to people to fulfil your ministry and thereby create your wealth. Discover where you are sent and with what message and stay there.

REASONS:

From Genesis 26:1-6, 12-14, we discover that you prosper and become synonymous with prosperity when you go to, sow into, work at and stay at the appointed place irrespective of who was there before you got there. Like Isaac, you begin to prosper, continue to prosper and become very prosperous to the extent that the philistines [the indigenous people, the original citizens who were there before you arrived] envy you in your appointed place both of worship and assignment. But you are thrown out of the boat and end up in the belly of a whale as your accommodation like Jonah when you go where you choose.

REMEMBER THE FOLLOWING VITAL TRUTHS:

YOU ARE ONLY A SIGN WHERE YOU ARE SENT - YOU STINK WHERE YOU ARE NOT SENT
YOU SHINE WHERE YOU ARE SENT - YOU ARE DIM WHERE YOU ARE NOT SENT
YOU ARE A MIRACLE WHERE YOU ARE SENT - YOU ARE A RIDICULE WHERE YOU ARE NOT SENT
LIGHT SURROUNDS YOU WHERE YOU ARE SENT – WHILST DARKNESS ENVELOPES YOU WHERE YOU ARE NOT SENT
YOU ARE FAMOUS WHERE YOU ARE SENT - YOU ARE 'SHAMOUS' WHERE YOU ARE NOT SENT
YOUR FAME SPREADS WHERE YOU ARE SENT - YOUR SHAME SPREADS WHERE YOU ARE NOT SENT
YOU ARE FULL OF GRACE WHERE YOU ARE SENT - YOU ARE DISGRACED WHERE YOU ARE NOT SENT
YOU ARE CELEBRATED WHERE YOU ARE SENT - YOU ARE TOLERATED WHERE YOU ARE NOT SENT

YOU ARE A CELEBRITY WHERE YOU ARE SENT - YOU ARE A NUISANCE WHERE YOU ARE NOT SENT

YOU MAKE NEWS WHERE YOU ARE SENT - YOU MAKE NOISE WHERE YOU ARE NOT SENT

YOU ARE ACCEPTED WHERE YOU ARE SENT - YOU ARE REJECTED WHERE YOU ARE NOT SENT

YOU ARE A POSITIVE INFLUENCE WHERE YOU ARE SENT - YOU ARE 'INFLUENCED' NEGATIVELY WHERE YOU ARE NOT SENT

YOU ARE AN ANSWER ONLY WHERE YOU ARE SENT - YOU ARE A QUESTION MARK OR ARE QUESTIONED WHERE YOU ARE NOT SENT

YOU HAVE PROOFS OR RESULTS WHERE YOU ARE SENT - YOU LACK PROOFS OR RESULTS WHERE YOU ARE NOT SENT

YOU ARE A BLESSING WHERE YOU ARE SENT - YOU ARE A BURDEN WHERE YOU ARE NOT SENT

YOU PROSPER WHERE YOU ARE SENT - YOU ARE A BEGGAR WHERE YOU ARE NOT SENT

YOU ARE AN AMAZEMENT WHERE YOU ARE SENT - YOU ARE AN AMUSEMENT WHERE YOU ARE NOT SENT

YOU ARE FULL OF FRAGRANCE WHERE YOU ARE SENT – YOU ARE A STENCH WHERE YOU ARE NOT SENT

YOU ARE BLESSED, UNMOLESTIBLE, UNHARASSABLE, IMMOVABLE, UNTOUCHABLE, UNHARMABLE, UNSTOPPABLE, WHERE YOU ARE SENT BUT YOU ARE CURSED, MOLESTIBLE, HARASSABLE, MOVABLE, TOUCHABLE, HARM-ABLE AND STOPPABLE WHERE YOU ARE NOT SENT

YOU ARE A WONDER WHERE YOU ARE SENT - YOU ARE A WANDERER WHERE YOU ARE NOT SENT. That is why when the crowds saw what Paul had done, they shouted in the Lycaonian language, "The gods have come down to us in the likeness of men." (Acts 14:11) compared to Acts 21:38, '................art thou not that Egyptian who stirred up trouble.......'

Then in Acts 28:4-6, 'And when the barbarians saw the venomous beast hang on his hand, they said among themselves, No doubt this man is a murderer, whom, though he hath escaped the sea, yet vengeance suffereth not to live. And he shook off the beast into the fire, and felt no harm. Howbeit they looked when he should have swollen, or fallen down dead suddenly: but after they had looked a great while, and saw no harm come to him, they changed their minds, and said he was a god.'

YOU AMAZE PEOPLE WHERE YOU ARE SENT - YOU AMUSE PEOPLE WHERE YOU ARE NOT SENT - Daniel and three Hebrew boys amazed people in their place of assignment while the sons of Sceva amused people going where they were not sent

- Your appointed place is your only place of accomplishments
- 2 Samuel 7:10, 'Moreover I will appoint a place for my people Israel, and will plant them, that they may dwell in a place of their own, and move no more; neither shall the children of wickedness afflict them anymore, as beforetime,'
- Psalm 125 says in your appointed place, you become immovable.
- There is no comparing the planting of God with the planting of men – (Isaiah 61) The appointed place is your place of security, safety, peace, joy, stability, blessing, accomplishment and fulfilment.

- the moment you lose your passion, you lose your power to achieve. God will give you several things but there are a few things God will not give you - such as passion - it is man that supplies the passion, the drive to see to the accomplishment of his vision - that's why Habakkuk 2 said He gives you the vision but it is you that does the running - that is where the difference comes in terms of the output and results. We need people with a passion - strong emotions. We are building a people who are passionate about our assignment to add value to others, raising and developing selfless impactful leaders to make impact in every sphere of life.

Passion is defined by the Encarta ® World English Dictionary as:
1. intense emotion: intense or overpowering emotion such as love, joy, hatred, or anger - Try and play it with a little more passion.
2. strong sexual desire: strong sexual desire and excitement
3. intense enthusiasm: a strong liking or enthusiasm for a subject or activity - a passion for music
4. object of enthusiasm: the object of somebody's intense interest or enthusiasm - Orchids are my passion.
5. outburst of emotion: a sudden outburst of an emotion such as rage, hatred, or jealousy

Q: We may have the same vision but why do we have different results?

ANSWER: **Differences in results is a function of applied passion, not just passion; but applied passion.**

PASSION IS THE VEHICLE IN WHICH VISION RIDES TO ITS DESTINATION!

- **Where passion stops is where vision stops.**
- **The output of your vision depends on PASSION - Do you have passion?**
- **Do you have drive? What drives your actions?**
- What are the programs put in place to see to the effective progress of the church you pastor or ministry you lead?
- It is your passion that moves you to put profitable programs in place beginning with outreaches and various church and specialized programs/seminars that are being organized to ensure the growth of the church/ministry.
- **It is Passion which culminates in a desire for Personal growth** or personal development for the fulfillment of your assignment - this is very important as John 1:16 reveals. 'And of his fullness have all we received, and grace for grace.'

SO PEOPLE COME TO RECEIVE OF THE PASTOR'S FULLNESS:
- An empty Pastor cannot fill a church.
- A pastor that's full inside him cannot continue to Pastor an empty church.
- What fills him and is full in him is what flows out of him to the people.
- No church ever grows beyond the growth of the Pastor.
- That is to say if a church must grow then of necessity the Pastor must grow.
- It is the growth of the Pastor that sets the pace for the growth of the church.
- If you give a church of 1000 to a Pastor with the capacity of 100, the church will dance down to 100; in the same vein if

you give a church with a capacity of 100 to a Pastor with a capacity of 1000 the church will jack up to 1000.
- Where your personal growth stops is where your church growth stops.
- Of his fullness have we all received - so a Pastor must develop his capacity for growth; he must enlarge his heart for growth. IT'S ALL ABOUT CAPACITY!
- The size of your heart will determine the number of people you can accommodate. Acts 6:4, 'But we will give ourselves continually to prayer, and to the ministry of the word.'
- RESULTS: Acts 6:7, 'And the word of God increased; and the number of the disciples multiplied in Jerusalem greatly; and a great company of the priests were obedient to the faith.'
- SUMMARY: So, the Pastor is the number one factor; the vision will begin to drive him and the true evidence of your vision is your passion.
- A church grows off the altar of the PASTOR.
- A growing pastor grows a church.
- The Pastor is very crucial to why people are leaving the church and he is the reason why many people are coming and staying.
- When a pastor stops growing his church stops growing.
- A growing pastor will always lead a growing church.
- You can't convince anyone you have a vision when you don't have a passion to back it up.
- When passion goes to sleep vision goes to rest.
- Every vision hangs in the grave when passion is absent - that passion will propel him to fast, propel him to pray, to study, spend quality and quantity of time preparing his messages, cry out in the middle of the night for souls, etc.
- So you see, there are things that when you have a vision

and a passion for, you will not be told to do; you do them of your own volition because you know it is mandatory for the fulfillment of your vision and realization of your goals.
- There are things that you just find yourself doing because of your passion.
- For instance the reason a Pastor has to be advised to fast and pray for his church to grow is because he does not have a passion.
- There are things that just occur in a natural sequence because of your passion.
- You organize programs that are orchestrated towards growing the church and of course in the process you are also growing yourself.
- As he grows himself God begins to fill up the place.
- Where a Pastor's growth stops is where the church or ministry stops.
- God is more bothered about your preparation of yourself than about filling the room - it is as you prepare yourself that God will begin to fill it up.

V. The fifth is THE LAW OF TOTAL ABANDONMENT* where you abandon your all on the altar of sacrifice to fulfil His mandate. The apostles asked this fundamental question in Matthew 19:28-29, 'We have left all and followed thee, what will we get in return?'

Ministry is fulfilled through the Law of Total Abandonment - total sacrifice. There are many ministries that have left nothing yet want to fulfil the ministry that God has given them. (Mark 10:28-30; Luke 18:28-30) Until you abandon yourself to the Caller, and lay all on the altar, Ministry will not be realised.

The disciples said - we have left all and have followed thee, what shall we have then? Don't go outside what you are sent to do or else you will sink. Until you have left all, you may never fulfil your ministry. Until your life becomes a seed, the fulfilment of your ministry is not in view. Until you are totally abandoned to your calling, you cannot fulfil it. Until you are addicted to God and your assignment, the fulfilment of your Vision is not in view. **THIS IS TOTAL DEDICATION!**

VI. The sixth law is the Law of ABSOLUTE DEPENDENCY ON GOD* i.e. making God your only Source for accomplishing His mandate in your life. God is your only Source. This law is built on three scriptural philosophies.
1. Whatever God cannot do, let it remain undone.
2. Whatever God cannot give me, let me never have it.
3. Wherever God cannot take me to let me or may I never get there.

So, at every point in my life and whatever happens in my life, it is traceable to God. Every time you share His glory with anyone, you annoy God. Thank the One who is using them not them.
- **You are not sent by the people; you are sent to the people.**
- Don't go outside what you are sent or you will begin to sink. Faith taps into the Omni-potency of God in dealing with the limitations of man; faith is a universal currency delivering at the same rate or value all over the earth. God is big enough to meet all the needs of the ministry He has given us. That's why He told the disciples expressly to 'Greet no man on the way; salute no man, lobby around no man's resources; no core group in your church; carry no purse or scrip, not even your leaders.' - Luke 10:4; 22:35

- God is big enough to meet all the needs of the ministry he has given to me. (Philippians 4:15-19)

VII. The seventh law is the LAW OF DIVINE COMMANDMENT*

- We do nothing except it is commanded - that is how you get things done cheaply in life and ministry.
- OPERATING AS COMMANDED! ONLY OPERATING AS COMMANDED!

In Ezekiel 37, the prophet said, 'I prophesied as commanded', just did as commanded and God went into action. Ezekiel 37:7, 'So I prophesied as I was commanded: and as I prophesied, there was a noise, and behold a shaking, and the bones came together, bone to his bone.'

Ezekiel 37:10 says, 'So I prophesied as he commanded me, and the breath came into them, and they lived, and stood up upon their feet, an exceeding great army.'

- **When you operate as commanded, you are always in command.** The Commander is always backing you.
- OBEDIENCE TO WHAT GOD SAYS TO DO WITH THE WORD IRRESPECTIVE OF WHAT'S GOING ON IN YOUR LIFE OR AROUND YOU is all that matters with God and all that God requires of you to make you a living star.
- IT IS ONLY THOSE WHO OBEY COMMANDS WHO EMERGE AS COMMANDERS.
- IT IS ONLY THOSE WHO RECEIVE COMMANDS WHO GIVE COMMANDS - you cannot obey commands and not end up a commander
- ITS ONLY THOSE WHO OBEY RULES WHO BECOME RULERS - you cannot obey rules and not end up a ruler
- IT IS ONLY THOSE WHO RECEIVE INSTRUCTIONS WHO ALSO BECOME INSTRUCTORS [GIVE INSTRUCTIONS]

- YOU CAN'T BE UNDER A GIANT AND END UP AS A DWARF - where the elephant eats is where it gathers its strength; you cannot eat elephant's food and end up as a cat.
- IT'S ONLY THOSE UNDER AUTHORITY WHO EVENTUALLY EXERCISE AUTHORITY OVER OTHERS
- Its only those who are under the tutelage and mentorship of lords who also become lords. Jesus became the Lord of lords [us] who submit to His lordship [ownership and rulership.]
- Revelation 5:9-10 reads: 'He hath redeemed us.......and hast made us unto our God kings and priests: and we shall reign on the earth.'

You only move as He commands - Lamentations 3:37, 'Who is he that saith, and it cometh to pass, when the Lord commandeth it not?' If it's not commanded by God, no man can bring it to pass. I do as I see my father do. If you don't want to be stranded, operate only as commanded. Operating as commanded is what puts you in command. We took over the second floor of our office premises because He commanded from Isaiah 54:1-17 and because He commanded it, He has been paying for it and sustaining it ever since. You don't move your ministry to another city or country just because you think it is greener there. ITS GREENER ONLY WHERE YOU ARE SENT AND WHERE YOU WATER IT! BECAUSE YOU ARE ONLY A SIGN WHERE YOU ARE SENT – YOU SHINE THERE!

VIII. The eighth law is the Law of MENTORSHIP* – A close observation over the years has revealed that African leaders are only recognised after they are dead; it is an evil spirit. Leaders in Africa are only recognised after they are dead. By inheritance, they are victims of castigations, character assassinations, etc. That is why most people in Africa don't have mentors; nobody seems qualified to mentor them so they lead a mentor-less life and by leading a mentor-less life they never reach their fullest potentials because God has arranged men on your path to bring the best of you out of life. No man is an island in himself - Jeremiah 6:16, 'Thus saith the LORD, Stand ye in the ways, and see, and ask for the old paths, where is the good way, and walk therein, and ye shall find rest for your souls. But they said, We will not walk therein.'

- Show me any man without a mentor and you will never be able to trace leadership aura on his life.
- Every great leader is an offspring of another leader.
- Every great leader's making is traceable to another great leader. If you don't have any man that you are following, there may not be any man following you. GOOD LEADERSHIP IS BORN OUT OF GOOD FOLLOWERSHIP. GOOD FOLLOWERSHIP LEADS TO GOOD LEADERSHIP.

Hebrews 6:12 reads: 'That ye be not slothful, but followers of them who through faith and patience inherit the promises.'

The passage of scripture above shows us how to correctly identify a plausible positive mentor for your life. People have obtained what you are striving for or you want to obtain; look out for them, and try to uncover their secrets, follow them and engage those secrets in the pursuit of your own life. Despite his eighteen hours vision encounter with God, my father in the Lord was told categorically, "I will not have you go as others have gone; I will have hands laid on you according to Deuteronomy 34:9, 'And Joshua the son of Nun was full of the spirit of wisdom; for Moses had laid his hands upon him: and the children of Israel hearkened unto him, and did as the LORD commanded Moses.' and you shall be filled with the spirit of wisdom, i.e. don't lay hands on yourself - send for Adeboye. He will lay his hands on you and you shall be filled with the spirit of wisdom.'"

- Despite the eighteen hour long vision and talking with God, God still connected him to a human source through which he could receive those deposits. 20 years after he had been following Kenneth E. Hagin's ministry, God said to him in a vision, 'Pattern your ministry after this man, - Kenneth Hagin.' Over the years, he had desired, 'Whatever makes Hagin, Hagin, I want it. I want the serenity, calmness, the noiselessness and proofs of this man and his ministry.' Eventually at a campmeeting in Tulsa, while he was on the balcony, he heard, 'My son David, the baton has been passed over to you.'

King Solomon said in Ecclesiastes 1:9, 'The thing that hath been, it is that which shall be; and that which is done is that which shall be done: and there is no new thing under the sun.'

There is no race you are running that someone else is not holding the baton of already. Where Hagin stopped is where Bishop Oyedepo took over. Hagin had the faith movement of the first order and the faith movement of the second order was passed to my father in the Lord, Bishop Oyedepo because you believe in their God and what they carry. (2 Chronicles 20:20) Identify the carriers of what you need, go after them, learn from them, believe in them, their ministry and personality, receive them, sow into them and their ministry, pray for them and then partake of their grace.
- **The law of mentorship must be recaptured again.**

- If you don't have a mentor today, we cannot be sure of your future tomorrow.
– Mentorship guarantees the future of everyone.
ASK: Fresh oil! Fresh oil! Lord. Let not your head lack oil.
Isaac Newton said, 'If I have seen further it has been by standing on the shoulders of those who went ahead of me.'

IX. The ninth law is the Law of FOCUS*
Matthew 6:22, 'The light of the body is the eye: if therefore thine eye be single, thy whole body shall be full of light.'
1 Kings 20:39-40, 'And as the king passed by, he cried unto the king: and he said, Thy servant went out into the midst of the battle; and, behold, a man turned aside, and brought a man unto me, and said, Keep this man: if by any means he be missing, then shall thy life be for his life, or else thou shalt pay a talent of silver. And as thy servant was busy here and there, he was gone. And the king of Israel said unto him, so shall thy judgment be; thyself hast decided it.'

'As I was busy here and there he was gone.....' STAY FOCUSSED ON YOUR ASSIGNMENT! Don't be lured into the trap of: 'This is what they are preaching now, so, let's do the same.'
- Lack of focus can make you lose your ministry.
- The more focussed you are, the more fruitful your ministry becomes. Kenneth Hagin stayed with 'Go teach my people – Faith' to the last day. Billy Graham has stayed with the message on salvation for over six decades, and abandoned the suggestion to build a university even though the resources were going to be given him on silver platter. Oral Roberts stayed with the Healing message till the last day and despite the vogue of church ministry he never deviated to become a pastor.
- Because of the impact Jesus had on people, they tried to

crown him king. When Jesus noticed they were coming to crown him king he walked through them and stayed in his assignment. He stayed with one the reason for which he came, 'I am sent to the lost ones of the household of Israel' and so did John the Baptist. When he was asked if he was the messiah, he replied categorically, 'I am not.'

These examples should help you and I to realign our priorities and remove every distraction.

FOCUS IN RELATION TO YOUR MENTOR:
- Keep your eyes on your mentor/father in the lord if you want to stay focussed.

2 Kings 2:10, 'And he said, Thou hast asked a hard thing: nevertheless, if thou see me when I am taken from thee, it shall be so unto thee; but if not, it shall not be so.'

1 Kings 20:40, 'And as thy servant was busy here and there, he was gone.

- Stay on your assignment remembering that it is kings who run after priests not priests running after kings; so, don't run after politicians, they should run after you.
- You can't be a great pastor going everywhere. Sit on your job.
- Proximity does not matter - it's heart to heart that matters.
 - Fathers are coaches most times telling you what you don't like.
 - Be ready to accept shocks.
- A father can disown a son but a son cannot disown his father.
- Fathers can be Harsh but right.

- Anyone who talks against his boss it's because it's not his own father.

- Philippians 3:13, 'Brethren, I count not myself to have apprehended: but this one thing I do, forgetting those things which are behind, and reaching forth unto those things which are before,'

ENEMIES OF FOCUS:
1. Ambition mixed with vision
- Peter lost focus when he went back fishing.
- Ambition is what you want - vision is what God wants. This is like mixing oil and water. Matthew 4:1-11 (shortcuts)
- The world must know you for something. They wanted to make Jesus a king but He run right through them. They asked John the Baptist, 'Are you the Messiah; his answer was 'I am not.'

2. Wrong company/Bad associations
- Not everybody at the bus stop or airport is travelling so not everybody in ministry is going somewhere.
- Proverbs 13:20, 'He that walketh with wise men shall be wise: but a companion of fools shall be destroyed.'
- 1 Corinthians 15:33, 'Be not deceived: evil communications corrupt good manners.'
 - **Iron sharpens iron, not wood.** - Proverbs 27:17, 'Iron sharpeneth iron; so a man sharpeneth the countenance of his friend.'
- Psalm 1:1-3, 'Blessed is the man that walketh not in the counsel of the ungodly, nor standeth in the way of sinners, nor sitteth in the seat of the scornful. But his delight is in the law of the LORD; and in his law doth he meditate day and night.

And he shall be like a tree planted by the rivers of water, that bringeth forth his fruit in his season; his leaf also shall not wither; and whatsoever he doeth shall prosper.'

3. Ignorance of the contents of your assignment.
- Your prosperity is in your assignment so focus on your assignment.
- Find out what God revealed to you and stay with it.
- Ministry begins with and is sustained by receiving four major instructions. You must of necessity receive these from God before you embark on your journey/enterprise in ministry: They are namely:
a. Description
b. Inscription
c. Prescription and
d. Subscription.

The statement: WRITE THE VISION DOWN in Habakkuk 2 means:
1. Describe it
2. Inscribe it
3. Prescribe for it and
4. Subscribe To it.

SO:
- 1st of all **describe it – define clearly what the vision is**.

- 2nd, **inscribe it – write it down so you don't keep changing it because of circumstances**, so it cannot be erased.

- 3rd, you must **take a prescription from God as to the How**! God said you will pastor a church of 10,000 - you have the steps. Now, **wait on Him to tell you how. This is what you need to do so what I said will come to pass.** For you to be what you should be, take this prescription twice or thrice daily, hold this or that event weekly, monthly or yearly.

- 4th, **subscribe to it** - after you've received the steps and prescription, **act upon it; do it; subscribe to the prescription.**

- This ensures you don't sway from the original path.

SO YOU MUST BE CONVERSANT AND FULLY PERSUADED OF:

1. THE WHO: Who is the target? Who are you called to? Who is to be involved? Genesis 11:6, '….and the people is one; nothing will be restrained from them which they have imagined to do' and 2 Samuel 6. Also, who have you been called to? – Paul to the Gentiles (Acts 26:14-19) Peter to the Jews.

2. THE WHAT: What is the assignment? What is the target? And all this must reflect His image and bring Him glory. That of Nimrod and those in Babel was nullified because it was for self; it was aimed at bringing them the glory and not God. That is why God came down and interrupted their program.

3. THE WAY: [how to achieve it]. In 2 Samuel 6, King David initially employed the wrong way to carry or bring the ark back to Jerusalem even though there was a prescribed way as stated in 1 Samuel 5-7 which should have been studied by David the king before employing natural, physical, trial and error means using a cart to transport the ark resulting in Uzzah in trying to stop the ark from falling by touching it – helping God, being killed. King David eventually repented, wised up, found and followed the right way to bring the ark back. SO: Find the divinely prescribed way or you'll end up using a blunt axe, exerting human effort and energy to accomplish little [Ecclesiastes 10:10] wearing everyone out or even killing yourself or others.

4. THE WHY: Why did God make you a king, Saul [1 Samuel 9 & 10]? Why did God give you the vision you have? Why are you doing what you are doing? Why did He give you that assignment?

For example, He said to Moses to tell Pharaoh, 'Let my people go that they may serve me, worship me and sacrifice to me in the wilderness.' - Exodus 4, 8, 9, etc.

Solomon's reply to God's question in 1 Kings 3:3-9, 'Ask me what you will' 'Give me an understanding heart' – Why? '..that I may judge thy so great a people.' There is always a 'why' to everything God asks you to do - find it. It helps make the journey great, significant, fulfilling and keeps you focussed when others doubt and criticise you. It is because they don't know what you know or see what you see - the end of the tunnel - the eventual outcome and the number of people that will be blessed by your obedience. Hebrews 12:2 says, '… Jesus, who for the joy that was set before him, endured the cross, despised the shame and is now set at the right hand of majesty.' On the cross when Jesus beheld what they were doing to him and saying of him and to him, said to the Father, 'Father, forgive them for they know not what they are doing.'

If only they knew and in the epistles, Paul the apostle said 'if only they had known, they wouldn't have crucified the Lord of glory'. He also said of himself on his conversion that he persecuted the Christians out of ignorance; he did not know that in persecuting the Christians he was actually persecuting Christ. **Ignorance is killer!**

That is why we should know the why.

Genesis 2:5, 'And every plant of the field before it was in the earth, and every herb of the field before it grew: for the LORD God had not caused it to rain upon the earth, and there was not a man to till the ground. But there went up a mist from the earth, and watered the whole face of the ground.'

There was no rain because there was no man to till the ground. There is always a reason for everything that God does. If certain things are not in place, God doesn't do certain things because there is time for everything as stated in Ecclesiastes 3. In Genesis 2:5-6, because, there was no man to till the ground God sent a mist out of the ground to water the ground.

5. THE WHEN: There is a when to every vision that God gives to every man. [Habakkuk 2 – though the vision tarries, wait for it, for it shall surely come to pass]. E.g. Esther in the palace; Moses in the wilderness with Jethro – the Midianites; David in the wilderness; Joseph sold into slavery ending up in prison for the preservation of life [posterity] - Ecclesiastes 3:1-3. The timing and environment must be right for the manifestation of the vision or promise. Find out when. When the fullness of time came, God sent his Son.

6. THE WHERE: Where is God going to bring the promise to pass? In the accomplishment of very vision, all these six points or characteristics must be seen or satisfied just as it was in the scenario in Genesis 11.

- The who: Come let us – all of them of one language [vss.3&4]
- The what: let us build a city [vs. 4]
- The way & how: they had brick for stone and slime for mortar [vs. 3]
- The why: for a reason - we will not be scattered abroad [vs. 4]
- The when: let us build now [vs. 4]
- The where: a plain in the land of Shinar where they dwelt [vs. 2]

Don't enter ministry without a specific personal and ministry covenant with God. When you understand the covenant you have, you have confidence and boldness to summon your covenant to deal with demons and hindrances that stand in the way of the fulfilment of your divine assignment. If you are sent, you must know the covenant that comes with your sending. Moses knew 'I am that I am' was with him to back up his words. The apostles knew He would confirm the words they preached with signs and wonders. Jesus knowing He was sent by God was bold enough to say, 'the works I see him do is what I do also', etc.

In conclusion, I repeat: Ministry begins with and is sustained by receiving four major instructions and knowing the 6 'w's and 1 'h'.

a. Description

b. Inscription
c. Prescription and
d. Subscription.
e. Know the following six crucial points: The 'who', the 'what', the 'way', [the how] the 'why', the 'when', and the 'where'.

> Rudyard Kipling said:
> "I keep six honest serving men (They taught me all I knew); Their names are What and Why and When And How and Where and Who."

You must of necessity receive these from God before you embark on your journey/enterprise in ministry:

4. Know how to deal with your prophet.
- Don't desire to be physically close, rather let your heart be close.
- You may have too many people but not many sons; many follow but not many are sons. Only Elisha was a son out of all those students in the school of prophets.
2 Kings 2:7, 'And fifty men of the sons of the prophets went, and stood to view afar off: and they two stood by Jordan.'
- Don't offend them and if they shout on you stay humble - don't change.
- Focus on the man you are following.
- Your attitude should be: 'I am here to serve and learn and receive from him all I need to get to my destination.
- Don't get excited at Gilgal, Bethel or Jericho. Follow your leader to Jordan. That is where you are asked 'What would you have me do for you?' and that is where you have access to the mantle and double of what your father is carrying.

X. The tenth law is the Law of CONTINUOUS LEARNING*

– Those who learn more, earn more. Today a Reader, Tomorrow a Leader.

1 Timothy 5:17, 'Let the elders that rule well be counted worthy of double honour, especially they who labour in the word and doctrine.'

- It takes a studious life to secure a glorious ministry.
- It takes a studious life to secure a glorious career.
- It takes a studious life to secure a glorious destiny.
- Schooling gives you a certificate and credentials but learning makes you a leader and a fortune.
- Schooling makes you literate but continuous investment in literature makes you an impactful leader and creates your future.
- If you are not studious you are heading for shame.

Paul said in 2 Timothy 2:15, 'Study to show thyself approved unto God, a workman that needeth not to be ashamed, rightly dividing the word of truth.'

- A preacher who is not a reader will soon preach himself out. Romans 11:33, 'O the depth of the riches both of the wisdom and knowledge of God! how unsearchable are his judgments, and his ways past finding out!'
- That is why he said 'study'. Nobody ever comes to an end of a studious life. The greatest Pastor on earth today David Yonggi Cho of South Korea said he spends 75% of his time studying, searching, preparing messages whilst others keep chatting and walk dry to the platform. **It is important for us to know that it takes a studious life to secure a glorious ministry.** Paul said in 2 Timothy 4:13, 'The cloak that I left at Troas with Carpus, when thou comest, bring with thee, and the books, but especially the parchments.'

'.....but especially my notes, my parchments, my books.'
- He was a learner, a student of the word.
- If you are not a learner you never become a leader.
- Everyone who is taking the lead is a committed learner.
- If you cannot see beyond what others have seen nobody will follow you.
- There are those who read the Bible for fun while some read to learn. If you are not a writer you are not a learner - the lessons you learn must be documented. If you want to enter into a rest, in your ministry then you must labour in the word of God, the anointed books around you, you must invest in resources in expanding your knowledge base. Some have said if you want to hide something from a black man put it in a book. This became a common saying among the whites. Unfortunately many have never read a book since they left school - we must enforce a change in that mentality. Schooling gives you a certificate, a job and credentials. But, Continuous learning makes you a leader and a fortune. What you do after school determines who and what you become. **Without a functional library you cannot generate extraordinary results or live an extraordinary life.**

Jesus was a perpetual learner. Isaiah 50:4, 'The Lord GOD hath given me the tongue of the learned, that I should know how to speak a word in season to him that is weary: he wakeneth morning by morning, he wakeneth mine ear to hear as the learned.'
……………..he was constantly learning at the feet of the Father. If you must become a great leader then you better become an addicted learner. The man Daniel even though endowed by God with wisdom, was an addicted learner. He said in Daniel 9:2, 'In the first year of his reign I Daniel understood by books

the number of the years, whereof the word of the LORD came to Jeremiah the prophet, that he would accomplish seventy years in the desolations of Jerusalem.'

- If you are not a friend of books, you cannot go far; do not be slothful………
- Have a functional library, not a decorational or decorative library.
- Have an appetite for knowledge.
- Have and maintain and insatiable crave for knowledge.
- If you are not a hard worker, you cannot be a high flier. You can't eat your cake and have it.
- There are too many lazy people in the pulpits today, who are only just having fun with religion and are not impacting any lives because they are not willing to pay the price. NOTE: The price determines the prize.
THE PRICE YOU PAY=THE PRIZE YOU EARN!
- The Law of tireless learning, the law of addiction to knowledge - an addiction to learning.
- If you are not a reader, you cannot be a leader.
- What you do not have, you cannot give. It is said that, TL Osborn in his latter days, turned his swimming pool into a library; Kenneth Hagin always had a book on his table before he went to be with the Lord; he was always reading. **What you don't have you cannot give - so sit up. There is no future for an idle man, no not in the ministry.**
- Double honour is a product of double commitment to a studious life. The more committed you are to a studious life, the more glorious your ministry becomes. A disciplined life orders his life. It was George Washington who said, 'Discipline is the soul of an army; it makes small numbers formidable, procures success to the weak and confers esteem to all.'

XI. The eleventh law is the Law of DISCIPLINE*

"Self-discipline is the ability to make yourself do what you should do, when you should do it, whether you feel like it or not." - Elbert Hubbard, author and lecturer

- Looking at the life of Paul the apostle, a profound leader, we see a clear display of the virtues of self-discipline. He said in 1 Corinthians 6:12, 'All things are lawful unto me, but all things are not expedient: all things are lawful for me, **but I will not be brought under the power of any.**' Then in 1 Corinthians 10:23, he said, 'All things are lawful for me, but all things are not expedient: all things are lawful for me, **but all things edify not.**' [Not all things are beneficial]

The word expedient is described as appropriate: appropriate, advisable, or useful in a situation that requires action or advantageous: advantageous for practical rather than moral reasons. **So, some things don't have to be morally wrong to be the wrong thing to do.** It's just inappropriate, inadvisable, not useful or advantageous for practical reasons more than moral reasons.

- A disciplined life places greater value on essentials.
- It orders its priorities intelligibly.
- It operates by schedule.
- It functions without requiring supervision.
- It makes the most of his time.
- It takes discipline to be distinguished.
- If you leave your life to chance, you don't have a chance.

"Without discipline there is no life at all." - Katharine Hepburn

- If you operate by whatever comes your way, you don't get anything accomplished by the end of any day. Discipline runs a schedule that tells him what time he gets up, what he does

between the first and second hour, what he does between the second and third hour, the third and fourth hour, fifth and sixth hour, etc.
- A disciplined person RUNS A SCHEDULE THAT CONNOTES A MAN ON A MISSION.
- Someone once asked my spiritual father, 'How do you get time to read?' He answered with a question, 'How do you get time to eat?' He continued, 'How can you schedule your eating time without scheduling your reading time or praying time or study time?'
- Discipline puts you on a lifestyle of schedules.
- You know what each day is supposed to deliver and you work at it conscientiously. So no matter where you are today, discipline can transform your destiny. The students who fail in school, failed not because they are poor, they failed because they are disorganized, they are disorderly, don't have an orderly program and do things as it happens.
- You never find a distinguished man who is not disciplined. It takes an orderly life to enjoy progress. Paul said I will remain committed only to what things are expedient. I will do only those things that are expedient. That is the law of Discipline.

XII. The twelfth law is the Law of DILIGENCE - HARD WORK*

Proverbs 22:29, 'Seest thou a man diligent in his business? he shall stand before kings; he shall not stand before mean men.'

Observe closely a man who is diligent in his business work - he shall stand before kings – not ordinary men - he has a place on top, not at the bottom. **So to move from where you are to a higher plain you have to take a flight of diligence.**

That simply translates as hard work. Jesus said I must work the works of him that sent me. John 5:17 says, 'But Jesus answered them, My Father worketh hitherto, and I work.' Paul said, 'But by the grace of God I am what I am: and his grace which was bestowed upon me was not in vain; but I laboured more abundantly than they all: yet not I, but the grace of God which was with me.' - 1 Corinthians 15:10

- You cannot get out of life more than what you are willing to invest into it. Paul said I laboured more abundantly than them all. The Law of Diligence - It is the only way to gain prominence in your field. 'Whatsoever a man sows, that is what he would reap…..bountifully.'
- Galatians 6:6-10, 'Let him that is taught in the word communicate unto him that teacheth in all good things. Be not deceived; God is not mocked: for whatsoever a man soweth, that shall he also reap. For he that soweth to his flesh shall of the flesh reap corruption; but he that soweth to the Spirit shall of the Spirit reap life everlasting. And let us not be weary in well doing: for in due season we shall reap, if we faint not. As we have therefore opportunity, let us do good unto all men, especially unto them who are of the household of faith.'
- Don't just carry a title, accomplish your task.
- There is no entitlement in titles.
- There is only entitlement in accomplishments.
- Don't just carry a title; Strive to accomplish your mandate.
- Your mandate is more important than your title - too many people are too relaxed to fulfil their ministry. Amos 6:1 warns, 'woe unto them that are at ease in Zion.' It is the only way.

Luke 12:49-50, 'I am come to send fire on the earth; and what will I, if it be already kindled? But I have a baptism to be baptized with; and how am I straitened till it be accomplished!'

- How am I stretched until it is accomplished! If your ministry does not stretch you, it will not impact lives - it is the stretching of your mandate that impacts the people under your ministry.
- The Law of diligence simply means hard work.
- Every minister you see who keeps moving about every day greeting people in the corner, they don't make much out of life. It is time to stretch yourself to deliver your mandate. There must be a Baptism of Labour. There is no way to give birth as a woman without going through the labour ward. You can't deliver your mandate without passing through the labour room of your ministry - you must pass through the labour room before you can deliver. Your mandate will remain as pregnancy until you go to the labour room. (Isaiah 66) Jesus said, 'I must work the works of him that sent me….' Paul said I laboured more abundantly than them all and the effect of his labour in his ministry is still speaking today. If Jesus tarries may the effect of your labour in ministry still be felt and be speaking four generations after you.

John D. Rockefeller said, 'When work goes out of fashion, civilisation will totter and fall.' That is when work goes out of fashion - when people devise short cuts to getting results outside work, advancements will cease. It takes work for things to keep working. I laboured more….but not me but grace. It takes grace to make the most of your time. We receive the grace to work and fulfil our mandate. (Proverbs 14:23; 12:24; 13:4)
- If you are not a hard worker today, you are sure to become a beggar tomorrow. My father in the Lord made this statement: "One disease that God has not cured in my life is the disease of being busy. Everybody even my enemies and the devil

knows I am very busy and my being busy is not to be regretted. Receive that grace today in the name of Jesus. I have seen proofs. We have crossed the $1,000,000 mark as wages today in Africa. In all labour there is profit. He that tilleth his land shall be satisfied with bread. Stay on your job - God is all you need to have all your needs met. If you don't want to become a beggar, please become a genuine worker.' (Psalm 1:1-3)

XIII. The thirteenth law is the Law of SPIRITUAL IMPACT*

- This is the source of your wages in the ministry.
- This is the source of your income in the ministry.
- This is the source of your livelihood in the ministry.

How Does A Minister Secure His Sure Continual Flow of Wages?

Romans 15:27, 'It hath pleased them verily; and their debtors they are. For if the Gentiles have been made partakers of their spiritual things, their duty is also to minister unto them in carnal things.'

1. Make your hearers partakers of your spiritual things i.e. what you teach and he will make it their duty to also minister to you out of their material things.

So, when you impact people spiritually, God makes it their duty to respond to you materially.

Deuteronomy 25:4, 'Thou shalt not muzzle the ox when he treadeth out the corn.'

1 Corinthians 9:9, 'For it is written in the law of Moses, Thou shalt not muzzle the mouth of the ox that treadeth out the corn. Doth God take care for oxen?'

1 Timothy 5:18, 'For the scripture saith, Thou shalt not muzzle

the ox that treadeth out the corn. And, The labourer is worthy of his reward.'
- The ox that is threshing the corn is entitled to the proceeds.
- The quality of your spiritual impact is what determines the material returns that gravitate to you.

2. Preach and show the glad tidings

Luke 8:1-3 records what happened in Jesus' Ministry. 'And it came to pass afterward, that he went throughout every city and village, **preaching and showing** the glad tidings of the kingdom of God: and the twelve were with him, And certain women, which had been healed of evil spirits and infirmities, Mary called Magdalene, out of whom went seven devils, And Joanna the wife of Chuza Herod's steward, and Susanna, and many others, which ministered unto him of their substance.'

Because their lives were spiritually impacted, Mary Magdalene out of whom seven demons were driven out and the others ministered to Jesus out of their own substance, not their leftovers. So, it takes spiritual impact to enjoy material comfort. So if you must have your wages, bible says the labourer is worthy of his wages, labour in the word, labour in prayer, impact the lives of men positively and they will respond gladly by investing in the ministry God has given you and invest into your life. All biblical laws are universal - they deliver at the same rate everywhere; whether you are in a village or city it will still work. It is a law.
- It takes a spiritual man to impact people spiritually.
- A carnal man cannot impact people spiritually.
- It takes spiritual men to impact people spiritually - it takes spiritually-minded people to impact people spiritually. That is why the Bible says to be spiritually minded is peace and to

be carnally-minded is death.
- You are either spiritual or carnal - you cannot be neutral.
- A Pastor who is stealing church money, how spiritual is that?
- A pastor planning how to break the church - how spiritual is that?
- A pastor who never prays or reads his Bible, how spiritual is that?
- A pastor who is doing politics or is involved in gossip with the congregation or creating factions or tribalism, how spiritual is that?
- Therefore every minister is his worst enemy - there is nobody that is against you as much as you are against yourself. When you do what you must do, you will see how weak the devil is. Therefore, there is nobody who is doing you - you are doing yourself. So invest in yourself and in your ministry - read, study your bible, prepare and eat your messages before you dish it out to others.

In 1987, God said to my spiritual father, 'Don't raise money; raise men and you will have more money than you will ever require for ministry.'

Today the vogue is about raising money, bringing in 'Experts' in raising funds. If your ministry is a men-raising ministry you will never lack money or resources. Put these things before your eyes, and as you do these things and live by these laws, your 100 members will become 200 then 400 then 1000 then 10,000 then 50,000.

- The testimonies of changed lives are the cheapest way to grow a church.
- It is interesting to note that: Publicity does not grow a church
- it is transformation [of lives] that grows a church.
- Raise men - the law of spiritual impact.

- They must have seen enough proofs to convince themselves that where the church is located is not far.
- There is no scientific strategy for growing a church. Once I was blind, now I see and that is why you must strive to impact the people spiritually and as changes occur in their lives, you find members of their family coming in, friends coming up, colleagues coming in and then the church is filling up.
- It is the Testimony of changed lives that grows a church, not, radio, newspaper or TV adverts.
- The growth of the church is effected by the members of the church whose lives have been touched and they go and tell others, 'come and see, we were all on the floor together but we are different now, come and see.'
- So, go every morning when you are going to minister to the people with a heart willing to impart to impact the people and you will see how the church will be growing. They go and tell the others, 'come and see' and that is enough TV advert.

3. Stay with your assignment – (Proverbs 27:8, 23-27**)**
Proverbs 27:8, 'As a bird that wandereth from her nest, so is a man that wandereth from his place.'

4. Know the state of your flock: Proverbs 27:23-27, 'Be thou diligent to know the state of thy flocks, and look well to thy herds. For riches are not for ever: and doth the crown endure to every generation? The hay appeareth, and the tender grass showeth itself, and herbs of the mountains are gathered. The lambs are for thy clothing, and the goats are the price of the field. And thou shalt have goats' milk enough for thy food, for the food of thy household, and for the maintenance for thy maidens.'

5. FEED THEM the Word - Preach and show the glad tidings of the kingdom. Galatians 6:6 says, 'Let him [them] that is taught in the word communicate unto him [them] that teacheth in all good things.'

The amplified version reads, 'Let him that receives instruction in the word of God share all good things with his teacher [contributing to his support.]'

So, the people are only permitted to minister of their material substance to those who teach good things. Not to come out of church downcast but rather lifted, because light has shined from heaven and their prison bands have been broken, walking free. So it is God who moves men. He said, 'if they minister to you spiritual things, it is your duty to minister to them of your physical or material things.' **So, you must generate spiritual impact in order to enjoy material supplies.** (Romans 15:27; 1 Corinthians 9:11)

QUALIFYING FOR, PROVOKING AND ENJOYING HEAVENLY SUPPLIES – 21 THINGS TO NOTE AND DO:

1. If you want to enjoy heavenly supplies, you must constantly generate spiritual impact.
2. If you minister to them spiritual things, He makes it their duty to minister to you of their carnal or material things.
3. If you make it your duty to minister to them spiritually, God will make it their duty to minister to you of their carnal or material substance or blessing.
4. That is why a man of God should be fully set for his meetings; people have real problems. FACE REALITIES: ASK yourself, 'Am I imparting the people spiritually or am I just having fun; am I getting at the people, are they being transformed and is it being backed with signs and

wonders in their lives?'
5. You must be so prepared, fed and set for your meetings that when you get there they can see the freshness.
6. Be forever committed to your preparations; as you appear and whilst you are teaching, eat the things you're teaching because you've been in strong fellowship with the Holy Spirit in preparing yourself to be an agent that will meet the needs of the people.
7. They must see God through what you are teaching, preaching and showing - that takes a lot of responsibility.
8. Great men and women of God package their lives to affect the people they are going to minister to. Package your life to affect the people you are going to minister to. Don't carry fun all about. Be in league with God. Be in link with God. Be in touch with Heaven so much so that within 15 minutes of your ministering, things begin to happen in the form of transformation of lives and manifestations of the Holy Spirit in the form of signs and wonders.
9. Spend time with Him before ministering.
10. LIFE DOES NOT GIVE YOU WHAT YOU DESERVE BUT WHAT YOU DEMAND AND WORK FOR. Life comes with a great responsibility. Am I touching the people? If I am not touching them, they won't touch me.

    Everyone in our various ministries today are great potentials for the kingdom depending on how we are touching them with truth and indeed. Touching them with spiritual values and that continues to enhance their values in life.
11. Prepare and Minister with great responsibility that people will be so committed by what they experience that they would want to stay till they die in your church.
12. Preaching and showing will continue to multiply the

number and multiply the resources. Acts 6:7, 'And the word of God increased; and the number of the disciples multiplied in Jerusalem greatly;............'

13. Preaching and showing - A ministry of proofs commanding divine provisions and divine supplies. You may say, 'I don't have the gift of miracles, signs and wonders.' God has given you a word. You are a steward of spiritual things. Every minister has been given the word; let that word begin to transform lives of the people and they'll begin to touch your ministry in very unique fashions.

14. These spiritual truths will work anywhere. Some say, 'O the people in this nation are.......' If it is the word, it will work everywhere. It cannot be broken by climate or colour. The scriptures cannot be broken. Deuteronomy 2:36 confirms this: 'From Aroer, which is by the brink of the river of Arnon, and from the city that is by the river, even unto Gilead, **there was not one city too strong for us: the LORD our God delivered all unto us:'**

15. **NO NATION IS TOO STRONG TO RESIST THE POWER OF THE GOSPEL** (Romans 1:16) Our master responsibility is our commitment to the Word of God because it is the baseline for transformations and the baseline for manifestations. Mark 16:15-20 says, '....God was working with them confirming the WORD with signs following.' It is the word that transforms and it is the word that is also confirmed to generate miracles.

16. THEREFORE: Preach the word in season and out of season and then you will enjoy great supplies for every heavenly mandate that you secure. Facilities are built or purchased through money and money doesn't drop on the altar or pulpit or on the floor; money always drops through human hands and it drops through human hands as they

are touched. HUMAN SPONSORS HIJACK AND LIMIT THE MOVE OF GOD!

17. Ministry is not financed by any marketing strategy; you can't market the church through getting public relations experts to use carnal strategies to market the church. He came and flushed out all who were buying and selling. You can't market the church; you can only operate by the truth to command results. Stop looking for carnal strategies to obtain spiritual backing.

18. THIS IS THE TRUTH: If you touch the three people, they will soon become ten and if you touch the ten, their lives will change from one pound to ten pounds and if you touch the ten, their lives will change from ten pounds to hundred pounds and as you keep touching them they keep multiplying in number and multiplying in favour and your ministry begins to go up and up. The strategy hasn't changed - the word of God liveth and abideth forever. The same strategy – the same Lord over all is rich unto all (Romans 10:12). As we remain in covenant with God and with each other, our stories will get brighter and brighter by the day, Amen! Go and preach and show; the iron bars will not stop us. RESULT: GOD WILL COMMAND ANGELS, ANIMALS, FISHES, MEN, ORGANISATIONS, PEOPLE WHO KNOW OR DON'T KNOW YOU, people who love you, hate you or dislike you to give to you. God commanded a raven and widow to feed Elijah, Joseph of Arimathaea giving his tomb for Jesus' burial; Luke 8:1-3; Abimelech and Abraham, Lydia; 1 Cor. 9

God is responsible for His servants' upkeep and wellbeing. (Luke 22:35)

19. The Holy Spirit will make it His responsibility to command and employ the ones you touch, impact, feed, lead,

teach, care for, the members to bless you financially with monetary gifts. (1Timothy 5:17 amplified version)

This is an area where many Christians miss God completely, because they view the giving of financial gifts as a loss instead of the opportunity to attract prosperity that He designed it to be. Some don't even consider that their minister is spiritually employed, and as such deserving of wages, gifts, honorariums and bonuses. It is amazing to me that when these advantages are given in the corporate sector no one murmurs or complains. However Christians very often begrudge the man of God the right to benefit financially from preaching and teaching the Word. (1 Timothy 5:18)

20. Those who labour as shepherds tending Christ's sheep should be paid by God through those they lead. Just as you would not close up the mouth of the ox labouring to tread the corn (thus preventing him from eating) – neither should you stand in the way of your pastor benefiting financially from those whose spiritual needs he ministers to. As one in covenant with God, understand that when God tells you to do something, it's meant for your benefit and the area of giving is no exception. When you sow a seed into the life of your man of God, you are sowing even more seed into your own life. How?

    First of all when you give, the bible clearly states in Luke 6:38 that it shall be given back to you again, good measure, pressed down, and shaken together and running over. It's truly beneficial for you to plant your seed (finances) into good soil (your man of God) because in obeying the word of God you will definitely reap a harvest.

21. In 1 Corinthians 9:7-14, it's absolutely clear that men of God are supposed to prosper, so don't look down on them

when they start to do just that. When you begin to sow and plant into their lives, you too will begin to prosper. Does your pastor preach the word with understanding, so that you can get a hold of those things God wants you to know? Does he preach what you need to know in order to be a fruitful Christian? If so the Bible says that man is worthy of the finances he receives. To hold back on financial blessing or monetary gifts is to go against the word of God and hinders your blessings in the process.

6. Teach the members to receive you as a gift from God – Ephesians 4:7,8,11-12; Matthew 16:13-end. Jesus gave you to them as a gift. James 1:17 says, 'Every good gift and every perfect gift is from above, and cometh down from the Father of lights, with whom is no variableness, neither shadow of turning.'

7. They must know you as their Pastor and know your wife – they must study your lifestyle as a Christian leader and follow your faith. [What you've been able to achieve with your faith] – 1 Thessalonians 5:12; 2 Timothy 3:10

8. They must Esteem you very highly in love and be at peace among themselves. – 1 Thessalonians 5:13

9. They must Pray for you daily both in the spirit and intelligently using God's word that you will behold wondrous things from God's word, [Ps. 119:18] that you will be delivered from them that do not believe and that signs and wonders will be wrought through you as you minister God's word and that the word will have free course and great impact. – 2 Thessalonians 3:1; 1 Thessalonians 3:2; Acts 12:1-17

[Peter delivered from prison] (Order my book: How to Pray and Why You Must Pray For Your Pastor and Your Church daily from www.houseofjudah.org.uk)

10. Teach them to Communicate to you personally – give to you willingly and of their own accord and corporately as a church and arrange occasional surprises for you. They endear themselves to God and you that way because a man's gift makes room for him and brings him before great men. They must stand with your ministry without reservation. – Galatians 6:6; 3:7; Hebrews 7:5; Philippians 4:14-17; Luke 8:1-3

11. Teach them to imitate you as you imitate Christ – be faithful to follow you. – 1 Corinthians 11:1; Hebrews 6:12; Philippians 4:9; 2 Kings 2:1-15; Hosea 4:9, 'And there shall be, like people, like priest: ...., and reward them their doings.'
..............Like priest like people.

12. Teach them to obey your teachings in order to be transformed - in the process, they will sow into your life – God will ensure it. (Acts 20:28-32; 1 Corinthians 11:1-2) A Pastor's number one ministry is the word and prayer, not running around. (Acts 6:1-7) As they serve Jesus and their Pastor well, Ephesians 6:1-3 shall be their portion. If the church will allow the Pastors to stay in the word and prayer, they will behold wondrous things and the members will increase, multiply in number and be blessed.

XIV. The fourteenth law is the Law of SOWING AND REAPING* [seedtime and harvest]: - The Law of seedtime and harvest is Key to **ENJOYING AN OPEN HEAVEN OVER YOUR LIFE AND MINISTRY** [Genesis 8:22; Galatians 6:6-10; Deuteronomy 8:17-18; Job 36:11]

- **PROSPERITY IS POSSIBLE IN THE MIDST OF SCARCITY. THERE IS NO RECESSION IN HEAVEN, IN THE KINGDOM OR IN YOUR CHURCH OR IN YOUR MINISTRY.**
- The Ministry's prosperity is different from the Pastor's prosperity.
- What the Pastor sows, he reaps like any member of the church and it is what the ministry sows that determines what falls on the ministry.
- The subject of sowing and reaping in relation to ministry has not been taught extensively.
- Many ministries are not involved in seed-sowing at all and that is why many ministries are financially strangulated.
- Many ministries are under financial pressures because they have not discovered the mystery of ministry seed-sowing.

On the 4th of September, 1987 at Sheraton hotel in Lagos, my father in the Lord stumbled on a mystery command in Hebrews 7:7 'And without all contradiction the less is blessed of the better.' When he asked what it meant, God told him, 'Let the ministries begin to sow seeds into higher ministries and as they sow into higher ministries, they'll begin to move higher in their pursuits. Begin to sow into higher ministries and see what I will do in the ministry.'

- **There are things you do as a matter of convenience but there are other things you do as a commandment** – this is not sowing into ministries in need but into higher ministries **because the less is blessed of the better i.e. having an established approach to seed-sowing to reap consistently by deliberate provocation motivated by purpose.**

REASON: COVENANT PRACTICE IS THE CURE FOR HARD TIMES! THE COVENANT WILL PREVAIL IRRESPECTIVE OF THE CLIMATE! THE COVENANT IS SUPERIOR TO ANY CLIMATE! OPEN HEAVENS IS NOT BY CHANCE! OPERATING UNDER OPEN HEAVENS IS NOT GUESSWORK OR BY TRIAL AND ERROR! IT IS CONSCIOUSLY AND DELIBERATELY PROVOKED!

DOES YOUR MINISTRY PAY TITHES?

Leviticus 27:30 says, 'And all the tithe of the land, whether of the seed of the land, or of the fruit of the tree, is the LORD'S: it is holy unto the LORD.'

- All the tithe of the land is the Lord's, it shall be holy unto the Lord; you shall not take an aught of it.
Malachi 3:8-12 instructs, 'Will a man rob God? Yet ye have robbed me. But ye say, Wherein have we robbed thee? In tithes and offerings. Ye are cursed with a curse: for ye have robbed me, even this whole nation. **Bring ye all the tithes into the storehouse, that there may be meat in mine house,** and prove me now herewith, saith the LORD of hosts, if I will not open you the windows of heaven, and pour you out a blessing, that there shall not be room enough to receive it. And I will rebuke the devourer for your sakes, and he shall not destroy the fruits of your ground; neither shall your vine cast her fruit before the time in the field, saith the LORD of hosts. And all nations shall call you blessed: for ye shall be a delightsome land, saith the LORD of hosts.'

Deuteronomy 12:14, '**But in the place which the LORD shall choose in one of thy tribes, there thou shalt offer thy burnt**

offerings, and there thou shalt do all that I command thee.' Malachi 3 says, bring ye all the tithe into the storehouse............... ....bring it where I shall choose.......

THE REALITY OF THE WINDOWS OF HEAVEN BLESSINGS

Enjoying an OPEN HEAVEN DIMENSION OF BLESSING OVER YOUR MINISTRY comes through tithing out to higher ministries and ministries you are instructed to give to. Our ministry sows ten percent of its income upward into higher ministries and senior men of God, spiritual mentors and my father in the Lord and their ministries that are higher than us and we attract the grace on them for speed and divine accomplishments. What you have to understand is the higher ministries you are authorised to give to don't need your seed - you are the one who needs and requires the grace upon them to fall upon you. Going around preaching to collect offering will not bring offering into your ministry. Stay on your assignment and the provisions will flow in. Start now - don't wait! Without an open heaven, your ministry will stagnate and suffer - that is the only way to increase - start now. That is how God has built himself ministries that are debt-free. Everything is debt-free and a proof of an open heaven.

Do you really want to experience an open heaven? Then, know and observe the following:

- Sowing into higher ministries takes you higher.
- Sowing into higher ministries opens financial fortunes to your life.
- Sowing into higher ministries opens you up into a new

dimension of financial fortune.
- Sowing into higher ministries empowers you to attract their grace.
- Sowing into higher ministries makes you attract their happenings, i.e. what is happening in their ministries.
- Sowing into higher ministries entreats the favour they enjoy.
- Sowing into higher ministries opens major doors of ministry to both your life and your ministry.
- Sowing into higher ministries brings speedy growth to your ministry.
- Sowing into higher ministries makes you attract what they attract.
- Tithing the resources of your ministry opens the heaven over it and you cannot be living under an open heaven without people noticing.
- Make sure you also give very good and worthy love offerings or honorariums to your guest speakers. It is absolutely essential, mandatory and crucial to the blessing that comes and remains on your life, ministry and members.
- There are Pastors who don't pay tithe. Pastors must pay tithes. The law of tithing is for everyone including pastors.

Galatians 6:6-10, 'Let him that is taught in the word communicate unto him that teacheth in all good things. Be not deceived; God is not mocked: for whatsoever a man soweth, that shall he also reap. For he that soweth to his flesh shall of the flesh reap corruption; but he that soweth to the Spirit shall of the Spirit reap life everlasting. And let us not be weary in well doing: for in due season we shall reap, if we faint not. As we have therefore opportunity, let us do good unto all men, especially unto them who are of the household of faith.'

- IF YOU ARE NOT A TITHER, I AM NOT SURPRISED THAT THINGS ARE TIGHT FOR YOU AND YOUR MINISTRY!
- IF YOU ARE NOT A TITHER YOU ARE NOT PERMITTED TO PROSPER!
- ALL THE SELF-PROCLAIMED 'MELCHIZEDEKS' MUST REPENT AND START TITHING NOW IF THEY KNOW WHAT IS GOOD FOR THEM!

Our prayer is that no one reading or studying this book will end up a beggar. I decree that every financial struggle both in your life or ministry comes to an end now as you practice this covenant of sowing and reaping. **Remember, it is not those who preach prosperity who enjoy prosperity; it is only those who practice the covenant of prosperity - seed, time and harvest** (Genesis 8:22; 12:1-3; Deuteronomy 8:17-18; Luke 6:38; Philippians 4:14-19; Job 36:11; Psalm 37:4-6) **who enjoy prosperity.**
[ORDER MY BOOK: GENERATING FINANCES FOR MINISTRY [WITHOUT SWEATING, BEGGING, TOILING, STRUGGLING, GIMMICKS OR RESORTING TO TRICKS] from www.houseofjudah.org.uk]

SECRETS:
1. Don't raise or receive offerings with an empty hand - an empty hand will reap an empty result.
2. If you are not a giver you are not permitted to prosper.
3. Stop raising offerings and start raising men and you will have more than you need to fulfil the ministry.
4. Obey these spiritual laws and you will be in command. Tithe!
5. The truth is that without money you cannot fulfil your

ministry and without an open heaven there will never be enough money to fulfil it. If money was crucial to Jesus and he needed a bag of money carrier [treasurer] to fulfil His mission, as anointed as He was, then you & I need it and the way to get it is by covenant practice.
6. You are a giver as a minister and a giver as a ministry [i.e. your ministry is a giving ministry too].
7. You are a tither as a minister and a tither as a ministry. [your ministry is a tithing ministry too].
8. The heaven will remain open and everything will begin to work and continue to work.
9. ADVICE: You should either give worthy honorariums to guest speakers or don't invite them at all; wait till you are ready or have an agreement with them before they agree to come and minister for you but don't promise and not deliver or abuse their gift. Let them know your size.

As a testimony: In our ministry, House of Judah, we set aside and sow ten percent of our income as a church to specific higher ministries and the results are evident each week. There is no stress in or on our ministry financially. God said after tithing, prove me now and I will open the windows of heaven and pour you out a blessing such as there will not be room enough to receive it. Grace to apply these treasures to your life – receive it now!

XV. The fifteenth law is the LAW of ENVISIONING [VISIONEERING] OR THE LAW OF IMAGINATION:
No matter your area of calling, what you cannot see today never becomes a reality in your life tomorrow.

In Genesis 13:14-17, He said to Abraham, 'And the LORD said unto Abram, after that Lot was separated from him, Lift up now thine eyes, and look from the place where thou art northward, and southward, and eastward, and westward: For all the land which thou seest, to thee will I give it, and to thy seed for ever. And I will make thy seed as the dust of the earth: so that if a man can number the dust of the earth, then shall thy seed also be numbered. Arise, walk through the land in the length of it and in the breadth of it; for I will give it unto thee.'

Many people have received visions from the Lord but they are not able to perceive the extent of that vision and if you are called the seed of Abraham, you are called to do the works of Abraham. **Whatever will become real in Abraham's hand tomorrow, he is required to see it today.** The question then is what seest thou? What do you see? What future do you see in the ministry that God has given to you? God said to Jeremiah, 'What seest thou? He said I see a rod of an almond tree. He said thou hast well seen I will hasten my word to perform it.' What you are not able to see, God is not committed to perform. What do you see? (Jeremiah 1:11-12) After the establishment of his heavenly vision in verse 3-7 he is called upon to visualize what he can see so he can become - what he cannot see he cannot have. We live in a dreamers' world - without a dream, destiny is doomed.
- What you cannot dream you never dare! It is the dreamers' world.
- Until you become a dreamer no matter how heavenly your vision is, it will be limited. The extent to which you can see is what will determine what will become of your vision.
- The law of imagination ...... though thy beginning was small

thy latter end shall greatly increase – (Job 8:7) that becomes your ultimate.
- So, a dream is a spiritual requirement for creating your desired future.
- See yourself talking to presidents, prime ministers, ministers of state well ahead of time.
- A dream takes you into the reality of your future before you arrive there - it is so intoxicating that it takes you there.
- It takes a sanctified dreamer to fulfil his ministry.
- It takes a sanctified dreamer to fully deliver the mandate of God upon his life.
- It takes a sanctified dreamer to make a full proof of his ministry.
- Declare what you want to see in your life and future.
- The future you cannot see, you never live in the reality of it.
- **A dream is the mental picture of your future.** He said in Genesis 11:6 '........and this they begun to do and now nothing can be refrained from them of what they've imagined to do.'
- So your imagination is what determines your destination.
- It is your imagination that determines your destination - destiny.
- '......for as a man thinketh in his heart so is he.' – Proverbs 23:7
- So what you think determines what you take.
- Whatever is too big for your mind is too big for your hand.
- Whatever your mind cannot handle, your hand will never realize. Whatever becomes of your tomorrow begins with your mind - it begins with your mind - it begins with your mind. Whatever is too big for your mouth to say will be too big for your hands to handle. **Some people are so busy thinking 'poverty' there is no way they can mistakenly step**

into prosperity. They think of poverty so much that poverty becomes their natural companion.

In 1986, just about the time his ministry started, my father in the Lord was asked by an American preacher, 'What needs have you in your ministry?' His answer was, 'Our ministry has no needs - we only meet needs.' He said he gave that answer because he just couldn't identify with the thoughts of poverty because his royal mentality had overtaken him. Nothing could be made to make him think poor. He said recently, 'The minimum seed we sow to other higher ministries is $5000.'

- You can't think poor and mistakenly become rich. For as a man thinketh in his heart, so is he. I am full of that mentality of stewardship under the King of kings and Lord of lords. **Until you can see a crown on your head, you can never wear one. Until you can see a crown on your head, you will never live to wear one.**

- I see you set free from day-dreaming; you are rather dreaming your dream from the Bible or day-dreaming. Jesus is the Sun of righteousness so whatever you can see from Genesis to Malachi to Revelation you are permitted to dream it; that is what is called sanctified dreams - dreams that are born out of revelation from truth from God's word. 'Seest thou a man that is diligent in his business he shall not stand before mean men.' (Proverbs 22:29) As a committed tither there is not one day that my tithe is missing in God's account, so I can only dream of open heaven blessing. If you want to walk in kingdom prosperity, you must walk in the reality of covenant prosperity through covenant practice. Do your part and commit Him to do His part. If you want to avoid shame in your ministry study, study, study, tithe, tithe, tithe, give, give, give and remain diligent.

- You can't be a sleeping and expect to be enthroned. No!
So, if you do not want to see shame, study, read, think, dream big, envision, be diligent, sacrifice, focus, be excellent and give it all you've got. That is the kind of sanctified dreams we are talking about. What has God said is obtainable and what has he said you should do to actualize it i.e. to make it happen. When you do what you must do, God's integrity is committed to make it happen. Sanctified dreams, revelation-provoked dreams, spiritually responsible dreams you have committed to make happen. There are many idle dreamers, there are people who dream of prospering without doing anything or what it takes to make it happen; so be responsible. Those are all idle dreams, balloon dreams. **What you see today is what you become tomorrow.**

- Don't be praying when you should be acting responsible. Destiny is a race of responsibility. If you don't want to end up a liability, accept responsibility today.

XVI. The sixteenth law is the Law of THINKING POSSIBILITIES

This law involves using your mind to create possibilities. **Think the word, think testimonies and think possibilities for as a man thinketh in his heart, so is he. (Proverbs 23:7)**

- Look around you and Use your mind. Everyone has a future but you have to begin to imagine it - see it. The mind of man is the birthplace of wisdom.

Bishop David Abioye said the following:
i. The mind can be described as putting your brain to work.
ii. You cannot become a head until you put your head to work.

iii. Those who use their heads cannot end up as tails.
iv. If you find yourself as a tail the only thing to do is start using your head. It is your head that puts you ahead.
v. Every slave remains in slavery until he begins to put his head to work - use his head.
vi. The cheapest way to terminate slavery and begging is to put your head to work. Use your head - use your brain.
vii. Sonship does not guarantee you automatic rulership. You have to be a son with a brain at work. (Proverbs 11:29; 17:2)

VARIOUS LAWS OF PRODUCTIVITY:

THE LAW OF CAUSE AND EFFECT: Everything happens for a reason. For every cause there is an effect, and for every effect, whether you know it or not, there is a specific cause or causes. (Proverbs 26:2) There are no accidents. You can have anything you want in life if you can first decide exactly what it is, and then do the things that others have done to achieve the same result.

THE LAW OF MIND: All causation is mental. Your thoughts become your realities. Your thoughts are as creative. You become what you think about most of the time. Think continually about the things you really want, and refuse to think about the things you don't want.

THE LAW OF MENTAL EQUIVALENCY: The world around you is the physical equivalent of the world within you. Your main job in life is to create within your own mind the mental equivalent of the life you want to live. Imagine your ideal life, in every respect. Hold that thought until it materializes around you.

THE LAW OF CORRESPONDENCE: Your outer life is a reflection of your inner life. There is a direct correspondence between the way you think and feel on the inside and the way you act and experience on the outside. Your relationships, health, wealth and position are mirror images of your inner world.

THE LAW OF BELIEF: Whatever you believe, with feeling, becomes your reality. You do not believe what you see; you see what you have already chosen to believe. You must identify and then remove the self-limiting beliefs that hold you back.

THE LAW OF VALUES: You always act in a manner consistent with your innermost values and convictions. What you say and do, the choices you make - especially under stress are an exact expression of what you truly value, regardless of what you say.

THE LAW OF MOTIVATION: Everything you do or say is triggered by your inner desires, drives and instincts. These may be conscious or unconscious. The key to success is to set your own goals and determine your own motivations.

THE LAW OF SUBCONSCIOUS ACTIVITY: Your subconscious mind makes all your words and actions fit a pattern consistent with your self-concept and your innermost beliefs about yourself. Your subconscious mind will move you forward or hold you back depending on how you program it.

THE LAW OF EXPECTATIONS: Whatever you expect, with confidence, tends to materialize in the world around you.

You always act in a manner consistent with your expectations, and your expectations influence the attitudes and behaviours of the people around you.

THE LAW OF CONCENTRATION: Whatever you dwell upon grows and expands in your life. Whatever you concentrate upon and think about repeatedly increases in your world. Therefore, you must focus your thinking on the things you really want in your life.

THE LAW OF HABIT: Fully 95 percent of everything you do is the result of your habits, either helpful or hurtful. You can develop habits of success by practicing and repeating success behaviours over and over until they become automatic.

THE LAW OF ATTRACTION: You continually attract into your life the people, ideas circumstances that harmonize with your dominant thoughts, either positive or negative. You can be, have and do more because you can change your dominant thoughts.

XVII. The Last and most important Law needed for us to fulfil our ministry indeed is the LAW OF LOVE* or THE LAW OF AFFECTION or THE LAW OF COMPASSION. It is also the law that puts us in command of all other commands (Matthew 22:35-39). Jesus finished a meeting and before sending the people away, he noticed they may faint on the way as they go in John 6:5-11 so he decided let's give them something to eat before they go. He said I have compassion for the people. His ministry was always riding on the wheels of compassion for the people.

Faith can get things done, Hope can inspire the people but only Love can truly impact people. Faith can get things accomplished, hope can get them inspired but only love can impact them. The 3 powerful forces in 1 Corinthians 13 are faith, hope and love but the greatest of them is love. **People don't care what or how much you know as much as how much you care.**
- You can inform them with faith, you can inspire them with hope but you can only impact them with love.
- It is only impacted people that can impact the ministry they belong to - only blessed people can bless the ministry where they belong.
- If the people you are pastoring are not positively impacted, they cannot positively impact your ministry.

Only blessed people can be a blessing. He said to Abraham in Genesis 12:1-3, 'I am going to bless you so that you may be a blessing.' Except people are blessed they cannot be a blessing. It is compassion that draws out your soul to another man or for another man's blessing. Jesus was always full of compassion.
- If you are operating with compassion, you keep enjoying expansion. e.g. As you are preaching, get one of associates to observe people, those feeling rejected, dejected, in pain and bring them to see you after the service - share with them what the church has. Until you do these you can pray till you die; they won't come near.
- Without a heart for people you cannot attract them. You cannot love people without them knowing. If you love them, they will know, because love is a spirit. God has not given us a spirit of fear but the spirit of love. People can pick it, because humans are spirits; they can always identify where love is.

Only compassionate ministers end up with great ministries. People that lack compassion are not entitled to expansions. Jesus had compassion for the people. He saw them as sheep scattered without a shepherd (Matthew 9:36) so, he went in and healed the sick. (Matthew 14:14) He would not let them go and faint on the way. Compassion will always culminate in supernatural manifestations. It is the compassion in your heart that works out the miracles by your hands. That was how bread and fish came alive. Compassion will always produce miracles.

You cannot have compassion and lack miracles. In the days of John Alexander Dowie, people were dying in his time and he was burying people in his church daily. He went into his closet and cried out to God, 'Lord enough' then Acts 10:38 exploded in his spirit and one of the greatest healing ministries begun.
....If you don't have compassion you are not entitled to unction. It is compassion that entitles you to the flow of unction. There are too many compassionless ministers in the streets. Too many compassionless ministers using people to meet their personal needs and that is why they are always in need.
- If you won't stop using people, they will soon leave you.
- Stop using people; if you stop using people, they will stop leaving you.
- If you don't have a heart for people they will soon leave you. A leper came to Jesus He touched him and soon leprosy left him.
- If you don't have compassion, you will use scientific facts to keep people deaf and dumb - keep people in their same state.
- Compassion provokes the flow of unction.

- Compassion guarantees expansion.
- If you don't want your ministry to suffer stagnation, then let compassion rise in your heart.
- Love is not a gift - love is a choice.
- Love is the choice of the wise.
- The greater your love for God, the greater your destiny becomes.
- The greater your love for people, the greater your ministry becomes.
- Love is a choice – a decision. After His resurrection, Jesus asked Peter, 'Simon, lovest thou me more than this?' His answer was: 'Lord you know that I love you' - so love is a choice.
- The greater your love for God the greater your future as a person.
- The greater your love for people, the greater your ministry becomes … there is no in-between out there.

Paul's heart: 1 Thessalonians 2:7-8 reveals the heart of Paul the apostle. 'But we were gentle among you, even as a nurse cherisheth her children: So being affectionately desirous of you, we were willing to have imparted unto you, not the gospel of God only, but also our own souls, because ye were dear unto us.'

- If people are not dear to you, you cannot go far in ministry.
- Your attitude should be: we are not just out to teach you, we are here to pour our soul to you……………..because you are dear to us. - That is what builds a great ministry.
- As a pastor of pastors, I see many pastors who don't have a heart for people; they are professional pastors who will halt anyone to have their way - the way they lead the ministries shows. You don't go far without a heart for people. Our attitude must be: we are not out there to take from you; rather,

we want our souls to be transferred to you; we want what we see to be what you see. We want you to be higher than where we are; we want you to know God the way we know God.

Someone asked my father in the Lord:
'What is the secret of the prosperity of your ministry?'
His answer was: 'When I bless the people, I bless them with the whole of my intestines; everything inside me is blessing them. God, if you will not bless these people, stop blessing me. We don't want to be called a fake prophet - so a ministry where only the minister is being blessed is a fake ministry. They are blessed people so they can be a blessing. It's a Church of blessed people. They are dear unto our heart.'
- If people are not dear to you, you don't go far in ministry. Pray, 'Let them have it; let them touch God more than I touch him now.' That will give you access to unlimited ministry. That may not be modern day ministry but that is bible-based ministry. Do you really have a heart for the people or are you taking advantage of them? When you have made a choice to love His people, the Holy Spirit empowers you to love more and more; the love of God is shed abroad in our hearts by the Holy Spirit. (Romans 5:5) **'I want the people I minister to, to be dear to me.** Lord, cause the love of God to erupt in my heart - I want the people I serve to be dear to my heart. Let your love spread out to people. Holy Spirit, cause the love of God to erupt in my heart afresh. Cause the love of God to spread to your people, Holy Spirit.'

- I see you and your ministry step into the realm of unlimited expansion. I see your ministry ushered into the realm of unlimited expansion. God has no problem working when there is no one there stealing the glory. It takes meekness to experience true greatness and growing greatness. Whatever we have seen God do in the ministries of our fathers, the living legends and also desire, we will see it duplicated in our churches and ministries and nations. It will erupt in our cities and nations. Amen!

3

ADDITIONAL PRESCRIPTIONS FOR FULFILLING MINISTRY

1. Ministry requires maintaining an open, humble, teachable and sensitive spirit – 'embrace' a correctable spirit. It will prolong your ministry and add excellence to it.

2. **Ministry demands that you Spend quality and quantity of time with God - that is what gives you weight, authenticity, precision, backing, undeniable proofs, character, power and longevity.**

3. Ministry requires the need to **REMAIN FOCUSSED AND PRESS ON TOWARDS THE MARK OF THE HIGH CALLING OF GOD IN CHRIST JESUS.**

4. Ministry requires dedication. Structure your life to fulfil

your Ministry. - Colossians 4:17, 'And say to Archippus, Take heed to the ministry which thou hast received in the Lord, that thou fulfil it.'

5. Ministry requires dedication to the following:
1. Study/Word time – 2 Timothy 2:15
3. Prayer time
4. Reading/Thinking Time
5. Family life / Recreation and Refreshing
6. Training/Personal/self development
7. Raising leaders/Delegation

6. In Ministry, you must surround yourself with people who love you enough to speak the truth in love to you.

7. Ministry requires you stay focussed in the Spirit Realm. - 2 Corinthians 10:4-6

8. In Ministry you must not run aimlessly Psalm 32:9, 'Be ye not as the horse, or as the mule, which have no understanding: whose mouth must be held in with bit and bridle, lest they come near unto thee.' Rather, do it objectively, subjectively and circumspectly. – Proverbs 29:18

9. Ministry requires ongoing training and being equipped both for your assignment and other people – not for your own singular purpose. Your life is not your own. - 2 Corinthians 9:10-14; 2 Timothy 2:1-2

10. Ministry requires you be a minister of Conviction – not convenience. Pride and Rebellion leads to Disobedience and Rejection. - 1 Samuel 15:16-23

11. Ministry requires courage and toughness to handle feuds

If you are offended by one thing, you will be offended by all.

12. Ministry requires you learn to exercise the Authority given to you for that Office.

13. Ministry requires focus – your undivided attention and input.

14. Ministry requires preparation for the long haul. Do not have a shooting star ministry. - Proverbs 3:5-8

15. Ministry requires absolute dependence on Source. Do not resort to gimmicks for your provision. Rely on El-Shaddai and Jehovah-Jireh. Jesus will impart instructions for your success/provision. - Philippians 4:19; 2 Corinthians 9:10; Psalm 84:11; Ecclesiastes 2:26; Luke 22:35

16. Life and Ministry is not fulfilled by intentions but by deliberate action motivated by purpose and passion backed by power and contention. (Deuteronomy 2:24)

17. No one takes this honour unto himself so you can't call yourself into ministry. (Hebrews 5:4) To call yourself into ministry is to live with endless struggles. Without a calling, ministry is more or less like a curse because it will be devoid of divine backing. Jesus said, 'Without me ye can do nothing.'

18. Ministry demands that you only say what He is saying: Don't lend credibility or credence to anything by saying, 'Thus says the Lord', if He didn't. – Lamentations 3:37

19. Ministry [It] has nothing to do with your expertise; it has to do with election and grace. If you are not called, you are not called.

20. Ministry is not a thing you desire to do but a thing you are called into.

21. Ministry requires excellence in who you are and what [all] you do.

22. It is one thing to be called, it is another thing to make sure that calling is realised. You must endeavour to make that calling and election sure from God's word and from practical experience. (2 Peter 1:10)

23. Ministry is quite an adventure made up of a lot of tests we must pass.

24. Ministry is a great profession and a profession requires skill and you learn this skill both before and on the job. We keep learning because when you stop learning, you start losing. That is the way up.

25. Ministry is not a journey of trial and error. Ministry is not a relegation to a life of toil, struggles and suffering but a life of definite purpose, dignity, colour, honour, unending proofs culminating in changed lives.

26. Ministry demands that you must beware of Err. (1 Timothy 4:1-6)

27. Beware also of the twin spirits in the last days - Seducing spirits and Deceiving spirits.

28. Be yourself in the Pulpit, don't try to be a Hollywood actor or else God will flush you out. (1 Corinthians 2:4-5)

29. God knows your hidden agendas – Don't be a freeloader

in the Ministry. (1 Peter 5:1-4; Hebrews 13:17; Acts 20:26-28)

30. Be a good custodian and under-shepherd of God's flock – you will have to give an account to God. (Hebrews 13:17)

31. Be delivered from the people. (Acts 26:15-18)

32. Ministry requires self-discipline.
- "The first and best victory is to conquer self." – PLATO
- "It is not the mountain we conquer, but ourselves." – Sir Edmund Hilary (first climber to reach the summit of Mt. Everest)

33. Seek not theirs [their stuff] but them [their welfare/wellbeing] - 2 Corinthians 12:14

34. Invest in your youth Ministry: A Strong youth ministry – grows into a strong church. Put emphasis in the Youth Ministry. (Eccl. 11&12; Ps. 127)

35. Vital Questions to consider for the preparation of a Ministry of Excellence.
1. What does God want me to do?
2. How is it done? (the way)
3. What will it cost?
4. Who will do it?
5. When will it be done?
6. Where will it be done?

36. Have a Vision, Goals, Dreams, Desires and Expectations – if not: a. People will perish. b. Ministry will perish.
REMEMBER TO ALSO Rehearse the Vision – Revise the Vision

37. Three Basic Conditions to fulfilling the Call:
1. You must have a desire.
2. Must follow through your desires.
3. You must pray. Ask yourself this question "What does God want me to do?" not 'What do I want to do?'

38. Set Goals
1. Planning – get your life organised around the will of God.
2. See lives changed **– yours included.** Only a life that has been influenced, impacted and uplifted can influence, impact and uplift others. John 1:16 says, 'And of his fulness have all we received, and grace for grace.' PEOPLE RECEIVE FROM THE FULNESS OF THE PASTOR
3. See nations changed for Jesus.
4. Purpose to plunder hell and populate heaven.
5. Pray without ceasing with Thanksgiving.
6. Focus / Think the word - Philippians 4:8; 2 Timothy 2:15
7. Fill your mind with God's purpose for your life. Dwell on it. Talk about it. Pray about it. Seek to excel in it.

39. Ministry requires Excellence, not Mediocrity. i.e. – All you are and all you have.

40. The Quest, strive for Excellence is Scriptural. Strive for the Masteries – lawfully. - Daniel 5:12; 1 Corinthians 9:25

41. In Ministry you must beware of and guard yourself against the three areas Ministers Fall:
i. Gold
ii. Girls
iii. Glory

42. Manners in the Pulpit: Manners, Ethics, Courtesy.
1. Punctuality
2. Brevity
3. Sensitivity and attentiveness
4. Duplicity
5. Credibility - Be honest, be real. - Psalm 51: 5-7; Psalm 139:23-24

43. Avoid Pride at all cost and handle and deal with every fallen situation individually.
- REMEMBER:
- No Leader is indispensable.
- God brings down one and exalts another.
(1 Samuel 2; Daniel 4:34-37; Daniel 5:25-28 - King Belshazzar)
- Saul was deposed and rejected, because of arrogance and pride. (1 Samuel 15; Psalm 75:4-7, 10)
- God is well able and knows how to humble those who walk in pride.

44. Give all diligence to make your calling sure. (2 Peter 1:5-8; Colossians 4:17) The DYNAMICS OF MINISTRY requires that you MAKE YOUR CALLING and ELECTION SURE – TAKE HEED TO FULFIL IT.

45. Fulfilment in Ministry requires your living a disciplined life. So, let's complete this section by examining the benefits of a disciplined life:
A Disciplined Life:
- Places greater value on essentials, not emergencies.
- Orders its priorities intelligibly.
- Operates by schedule.
- Functions without requiring supervision.
- Makes the most of his time.
- Makes one distinguished – stand out in his field –

outstanding.
- Does not leave its life to chance - you don't stand a chance that way.
- Is guided by a clear vision knowing if you operate by whatever comes your way, you don't get anything accomplished by the end of any day.
- Runs a schedule that tells him what time he wakes up, what he does between the first and second hour, what he does between the second and third hour, the third and fourth hour, fifth and sixth hour, etc.
- RUNS A SCHEDULE THAT CONNOTES A MAN ON A MISSION. Someone once asked my spiritual father, 'How do you get time to read?' He answered with a question, 'How do you get time to eat?' He continued, 'How can you schedule your eating time without scheduling your reading time or praying time or studying time?'
- Puts you on a lifestyle of schedules. You know what each day is supposed to deliver and you work at it conscientiously. George Washington said, 'Discipline is the soul of an army; it makes small numbers formidable, it procures success to the weak and confers esteem to all.'
- Transforms your destiny. The students who failed in school, failed not because they were poor but because they were disorganized, disorderly, without an orderly program and doing things as it happens. They failed not because they knew nothing; but because they didn't know enough.

FINALLY: You never find a distinguished man who is not disciplined.
- It takes an orderly life to enjoy progress.
- IT TAKES AN ORDERED LIFE TO GIVE ORDERS!
- IT IS THOSE WHO ORDER THEIR LIVES WHO GIVE ORDERS IN LIFE!
- IT IS THOSE WHO OBEY ORDERS WHO GIVE ORDERS!
- IT IS THOSE WHO OBEY COMMANDS WHO GIVE

COMMANDS!
- IT IS THOSE WHO OBEY RULES WHO BECOME RULERS!
- IT IS ONLY THOSE WHO RECEIVE INSTRUCTIONS WHO GIVE INSTRUCTIONS!
- IT IS ONLY THOSE WHO OBEY COMMANDS WHO BECOME COMMANDERS!
- IT IS ONLY THOSE WHO OBEY INSTRUCTIONS WHO BECOME INSTRUCTORS!

Paul said in the following passages of scripture:
1 Corinthians 6:12, 'All things are lawful unto me, but all things are not expedient: all things are lawful for me, but I will not be brought under the power of any.'

1 Corinthians 10:23, 'All things are lawful for me, but all things are not expedient: all things are lawful for me, but all things edify not.'

In other words, I will remain committed only to and do only those things that are expedient [appropriate and beneficial] for my destiny. That is why he said in Colossians 4:17. 'And say to Archippus, Take heed to the ministry which thou hast received in the Lord, that thou fulfil it.'

In the next chapter, we will examine the **CRUCIAL ROLE OF FAITH IN FULFILLING YOUR MINISTRY.**

4

FAILURE-PROOFING YOUR MINISTRY THROUGH THE FORCE OF FAITH

2 Peter 1:5-8, 10, 'And beside this, giving all diligence, add to your faith virtue; and to virtue knowledge; and to knowledge temperance; and to temperance patience; and to patience godliness; and to godliness brotherly kindness; and to brotherly kindness charity. For if these things be in you, and abound, they make you that ye shall neither be barren nor unfruitful in the knowledge of our Lord Jesus Christ......... Wherefore the rather, brethren, give diligence to make your calling and election sure: FOR IF YE DO THESE THINGS YE SHALL NEVER FALL: [OR YE SHALL NEVER FAIL]'

Beside this, giving all diligence…

That means: give these issues all of your attention it requires. The best way and best place to begin is the beginning. So: faith is the beginning; faith is the baseline for fulfilment of every vision.

Add to your faith... SO: You don't add faith to anything else; you add everything else to faith. Why? Because: Faithful is he who calleth thee, who also will do it.

Notice the words 'called' and 'do'. – 1 Thessalonians 5:24

- INFERENCE: IF He called you, He is obligated to do it.

- To get God involved, faith is required. Whatever will take God will require faith. Without faith it is impossible to [please] move God. – Hebrews 11:6

God's word says, 'If the foundation be destroyed what can the righteous do.' – Psalm 11:3

- Everything about God, everything about vision, everything about destiny, everything about calling begins with faith. Everything begins with faith and is sustained by faith. Hebrews 1:3 says HE UPHOLDS /UNDERGIRDS ALL THINGS BY THE WORD OF HIS POWER.

- Faith is the foundation for the fulfilment of every vision.

- Faith is the foundation for the realisation of every calling, election and destiny. 'Without faith it is impossible to please God.' – Hebrews 11:6

Without faith it is impossible to move God and without God it is impossible for you to accomplish your vision/assignment in life.

Jesus said, 'Without me ye can do nothing.' (John 15:5)

Scripture also says, 'It is not of him that willeth nor of him that runneth, but the Lord that sheweth mercy...' – Romans 9:16

Scripture also says, 'By strength shall no man prevail.' – 1 Samuel 2:9

IT IS VERY IMPORTANT FOR US TO COME TO A POINT OF THIS UNDERSTANDING that:

> Without faith we are bound to fail.
>
> Without faith we cannot get at God and without God we cannot deliver. Scripture says in Psalm 127, 'Except the Lord builds the house, they labour in vain that build it.......'
>
> Without faith we are building in vain.
>
> Without faith our ministry has no future.
>
> Without faith our future has no future.
>
> Without faith there is no future in our future.
>
> FAITH IS IT! FAITH is the only currency we must transact.
>
> That is the treasure at our disposal DEPOSITED BY GOD to bless our generation. Faith is a universal currency that delivers at the same rate in every nation of the earth. It is no respecter of persons or nations but those that engage or employ it.
>
> It has the same purchasing value in every nation of the earth.
>
> Absolute Faith equals Absolute Victory.

Absolute Faith equals Absolute Victory anywhere, any day and any time. Why? Because faith commits God's integrity and when God is committed, the deed is done.

When we get to a point of understanding of what faith is, then, victory becomes a way of life.

When we get to understand what faith actually means, victory becomes the only way we live.

Victory becomes a way of life when faith is actively at work in you.

- We have to be delivered from the world system, the belief system of the world, which promulgates faith in goals and faith in self like the statement: Believe in yourself! It does not work in the kingdom. King Solomon said in Ecclesiastes 9:11, 'I returned, and saw under the sun, that the race is not to the swift, nor the battle to the strong, neither yet bread to the wise, nor yet riches to men of understanding, nor yet favour to men of skill; but time and chance happeneth to them all.' WHY? In the Kingdom, COMMON SENSE IS NONSENSE!

Paul said in Philippians 3:3, 'For we are the circumcision, which worship God in the spirit, and rejoice in Christ Jesus, and have no confidence in the flesh.'

- Faith is a demonstration of confidence in God not confidence in flesh.

- Faith in God is what makes the journey great.

- Every outstanding thing or feat in the kingdom of God is a direct product of faith in God.

- Everyone has a beginning. Don't jump at the glory! Settle

down to understand the story. When you understand the story, it becomes easy for you to give the correct value for the glory. Until you are willing to change your approach, you cannot change. Many are exacting a lot of energy but you cannot accomplish a divine mandate in the energy of the flesh. By strength shall no man prevail!

- Every divine mandate has God's input as its guarantee… without GOD'S INVOLVEMENT EVERY MANDATE HAS NO FUTURE. (John 5:19; 15:5) WITHOUT GOD'S INVOLVEMENT NO MANDATE HAS A FUTURE. Without me ye can do nothing. Therefore, re-awaken your spirit man to realise that faith is absolutely essential. Faith is the fundamental requirement for your vision in God to be realised!

FAITH IS IT!

EVERY TEST IS A TEST OF YOUR Faith! PROOF: James 1:2 says, '… the trying of your faith, worketh [produces] patience [endurance]…' not the trying of you, but the trying of your faith.

If every test is a test of faith then we must put up a fight of faith.

If it is a test of faith, it will take a FIGHT of faith to OVERCOME.

Apostle Paul confirmed this in 1 Timothy 6:12, 'Fight the good fight of faith, lay hold on eternal life, whereunto thou art also called, and hast professed a good profession before many witnesses.'

SO: YOU FIGHT TO LAY HOLD – YOU FIGHT THE GOOD

FIGHT OF FAITH IN ORDER TO LAY HOLD OF [OBTAIN/SECURE] WHAT IS YOURS. NO FIGHTING, NO LAYING HOLD OF ANYTHING.

IN THE NEXT PASSAGE (2 Timothy 4:7) YOU FIGHT TO FINISH YOUR COURSE ON EARTH!

WHY? BECAUSE:

LIFE DOES NOT GIVE YOU WHAT YOU DESERVE; LIFE GIVES YOU WHAT YOU DEMAND! (Matthew 11:12; Deuteronomy 2:24)

LIFE DOES NOT GIVE YOU WHAT YOU DESERVE EVEN THOUGH IT KNOWS IT'S LEGALLY AND RIGHTFULLY YOURS - LIFE GIVES YOU WHAT YOU DEMAND IN DILIGENCE, BATTLE and CONTENTION!

LIFE IS A WARFARE NOT A FUNFARE!

LIFE IS A BATTLEGROUND NOT A PLAYGROUND!

That's why at the end of his journey, Apostle Paul could say in 2 Timothy 4:7-8, 'I have fought a good fight, I have finished my course, I have kept the faith: Henceforth there is laid up for me a crown of righteousness, which the Lord, the righteous judge, shall give me at that day: and not to me only, but unto all them also that love his appearing. ' SO: You fight to lay hold [OBTAIN] and you also fight to finish your course! THAT IS THE ONLY WAY TO TOTAL VICTORY!

WHAT MAKES YOU DANGEROUS TO THE DEVIL IS YOUR FAITH!

If EVERY TEST IS A TEST OF FAITH and you have to put up a fight of faith to overcome, then, without faith you are bound to fail. When Satan came at Peter in Luke 22:32, Jesus said, 'I have prayed for you, that, thy faith faileth not.'

SO THE ENEMY'S TARGET AND FOCUS IN YOUR LIFE IS YOUR FAITH NOT YOU PER SE.

Every test in our journey will require faith [the deliberate exercising of your faith] to win. Without faith, you and I don't have a future.

When faith fails, everything else fails.

Where your faith stops is where your life stops because the scriptures cannot be broken and those scriptures say: 'This is the victory that overcomes the world even our faith.' (1 John 5:4-5)

Bible says, God did test Abraham and Abraham prevailed, triumphed, and succeeded. (Romans 4:16-25; Genesis 22)

God's answer to him after passing the faith test was: 'Now I know.'

Whatever test it is, when you lean on God, you are bound to make it.

When you are truly connected to Him you are bound to make it.

It takes faith to make it work.

WHAT THEN IS FAITH?

1. FAITH IS NOT A PHILOSOPHICAL FACT - FAITH IS A SPIRITUAL FORCE.

- FAITH IS NOT AN INTELLECTUAL FACT - FAITH IS A

SPIRITUAL FORCE.

- FAITH IS A LIVING FORCE DRAWN FROM THE LIVING WORD TO PRODUCE LIVING PROOFS.

For example, the Woman with the issue of blood in Luke 8:40-46, came from behind and touched the hem of Jesus' garments and immediately Jesus felt virtue had gone out of Him and asked 'Who touched me?' So, her faith drew from God's living word [JESUS] virtue to produce living proofs in her life. Her faith drew virtue from the living word of God, which produced living proofs in her body.

So: Every time you come to a point of faith in God's word, you draw virtue out of it, to bring its contents to pass in your life. Every time you come to a point of faith on any truth of the scriptures, you draw virtue out of it to produce living proofs in your life.

- Every time you come to a point of faith in God's word, virtue is transmitted to you for performance.

- Every time you come to a point of faith, not when you think, but when you come to a point of faith in God's word [BECAUSE FAITH COMETH by hearing and hearing God's word] or on any truth of the scriptures in God's word, virtue is transmitted from the written word into your mortal being to produce a living proof to validate the contents of that scripture.

COMING TO A POINT OF FAITH ON ANY TRUTH LIKE WEALTH, DEBT, PROSPERITY, HEALING, LONG LIFE, etc. IS WHAT FAITH IS:

Faith is drawn from the living word to produce living proofs. From these scriptures: Joshua 1:8-9; Deuteronomy 15:6; 28:12;

Proverbs 22:7 I came to a point of faith on that subject which made me make a decision to clear my debts, never borrow or owe anyone. Something was drawn from that truth, a living force and virtue came out of that truth, into my being which made it impossible for me to do otherwise, resulting in a life of no stress, no strain and no indebtedness - THE WORD WORKS!

She came from behind, reached and touched Jesus' garments and virtue left Jesus' body into her body. She felt in her body that she was healed and the flow of blood stopped and the flow of her shame and reproach stopped. PROPHECY: The flow of your shame will stop when you successfully tap into this same virtue. In another passage of scripture in response to Jesus' instruction to launch out into the deep, Peter responded 'We have toiled all night but at thy word I will let down the net' and they caught a lot of fish and the net brake – living proof.

2. FAITH IS NOT JUST BELIEVING GOD; FAITH IS OBEYING GOD TO PROVE THAT YOU BELIEVE HIM SO AS TO COMMIT HIM TO PERFORM HIS WORD.

So, faith draws its strength from obedience to the word of God.

The force of faith is drawn from your obedience to the word of God.

Faith is not agreeing that God is Almighty – the devil also agrees and shivers – I know who thou art - Knowing who God is, is not equal to faith. Doing what God says is what faith is. Satan said, 'I know who thou art, thou art Christ the son of the Most high God' – that's not enough and that's not faith. Recognising that God is Almighty or God can do anything is not faith - that is simply a discovery.

Man shall not live by discovery, man shall live by faith (Matthew 4:4; Romans 1:17) – the just shall live by faith - his faith, not just by his knowledge or by his discoveries. The just shall live by his faith – so Faith is obeying GOD to prove that you believe Him so as to commit Him to perform His word.

Everything answers to faith and faith only answers with delight to every demand of the scriptures.

If you can believe, all things are possible to him that believeth. - Mark 9:23

That is: if you will do everything that is required of you on every issue, then whatever God says, you can be sure He will deliver it.

a. There is no magic about faith. Faith is simply the application of the word as it relates to every issue of life with which you are confronted.

b. There is no magic about faith. Faith is employing the word of God in dealing with specific issues of your life.

c. Faith is therefore not waiting for God to move – rather FAITH is moving for God to move.

- That is why: Any faith that makes God absolutely responsible for the outcome of your life is an irresponsible faith.

d. Faith is taking spiritual responsibility to provoke divine intervention.

- Knowing what God says is not revelation.

- Knowing what to do to actualise what God says is revelation.

- Knowing what God has promised is information but knowing

the conditions required for the promises to be fulfilled is revelation.

- So most of what we jump about calling revelation is mere information.

Jesus came face to face with a challenge. He had compassion for the people who had been with him three days and said if they went by that way they would faint on the way. So He told Philip to give them to eat by sitting them down in groups. Bible said, 'This He said to prove them for He himself knew what He would do.' (John 6:6)

SO: Revelation is, knowing what to do to bring God's hand to bear on any given situation.

Revelation is not: just knowing what God can do - that is information.

Revelation is: knowing what you must do for God to step in. HE HIMSELF KNEW WHAT HE WOULD DO - That is compound revelation - Jesus knew the scriptures in Psalm 67:5-7, 'Let the people praise thee O God, let all the people praise thee, then shall the earth yield her increase………..and God shall bless us and all the ends of the earth shall fear him.' Knowing this, He took the five loaves and two fishes and said, 'Father I thank you' and the earth brought her increase, and He gave to them; fed the 5000 men plus mothers and children and there was many leftovers, twelve baskets full – over and above.

PROPHECY: That is the rest God is bringing you into from this teaching on faith.

He did the same at Lazarus' tomb. Most people have been playing around with information, mistaking them for revelation and so we are victims of frustrations.

e. Faith is not standing on what God says in His word as it were. Faith is getting to know what God says must be done so He can move in to fulfil His word - that is revelation.

- Walking and living by Bible faith moves you into another dimension and positions you where nothing in your life or business or ministry is on credit. There is no indebtedness of any kind, no begging, no borrowing, no tricks, no pressure, no screaming, games, sweat, toiling, no stress or manipulation because you've found and seen [discovered] what to do and are doing it.

My father in the Lord, Bishop Oyedepo said, "Back in 1987, I found, I saw what to do to move into this dimension of prosperity. I discovered what to do about my personal prosperity (March 1981) and what to do about our corporate prosperity [27th August 1987]. I knew when it happened and He said, 'When you have found it, there shall be a reward and your expectation shall not be cut off.' When I found it, I screamed 'I found it, I found it.' I SAW WITH MY SPIRITUAL EYES THE THINGS WE ARE SEEING TODAY AND FAR BEYOND THE THINGS WE ARE SEEING TODAY. I SAW IT CLEAR. In 1981, I KNEW I CAN NEVER BE POOR just by knowing what must be done and I put myself on the line. I've never needed encouragement doing these things."

PROPHECY: 'Today, what you need to do to open the next chapter of your life and ministry, God will put it into your hand.'

f. FAITH is not just finding what God can do but locating what must be done in order for God to do it i.e. to actualise it. The Scriptures cannot be broken, not even by God.

- THE WILL OF GOD IS THE ONLY LIMITS OF FAITH: The Moment You Violate His Will, Faith Has Become Impotent.

g. Faith is obeying GOD to prove that you believe him so as to commit him to perform his word. KNOWING WHAT GOD CAN DO IS NO REVELATION! KNOWING WHAT TO DO TO MOVE GOD ON THE SCENE IS REVELATION! Jesus Himself knew not what God can do; He knew what He would do; He knew what He would do.

ASK/PRAY: 'Open my eyes Lord that I may behold the wondrous things out of thy law.' (Psalm 119:18) I know there is a way out of here to my destination; there is a way forward out of here. I know this is not where I am ending my journey; open my eyes to the world of revelations concerning the situations of my life; open my eyes into a world of revelations to what I must do for you to move; open my eyes Lord, open my eyes Lord.'

- There is always what you must do for God to move you forward.

- KNOWING GOD'S PROMISES IS INFORMATION

- KNOWING THE CONDITIONS REQUIRED TO SEE THOSE PROMISES FULFILLED IS REVELATION.

When they heard the message, they said, 'Men and brethren, what shall we do?' – Acts 2:38 REPLY: 'Repent and be baptised' - they did and then, they entered into a new world.

Acts 16:31 – Believe in the Lord Jesus and you shall be saved.

THERE IS ALWAYS WHAT TO DO IN ORDER FOR GOD TO MOVE.

Mark 10:31 – 'What shall I do to inherit the kingdom of

God?'

THERE IS ALWAYS WHAT TO DO FOR GOD TO MOVE.

Those are the wondrous, endless things that are in His law. They are the conditions that unfold what you desire and are the actions you must put up in order to see God in action.

There is nothing He tells us to do that is not within our power to do it.

Abraham stood out as an example of faith that works. WHAT WAS ABRAHAM'S SECRET?

God said to him in Genesis 12, 'Get out of your country…………….and so Abraham departed………..' Then, in Genesis 17, God said to him, 'I want to establish a covenant with you and your seed……' The same day Abraham took a stone and circumcised himself [a suicidal act] and his sons. Then in Genesis 22:1, 'Take your son, your only son Isaac whom thou lovest, come to a mountain that I will show you……and there sacrifice unto me for a burnt offering to me…' and the Bible says, '……Abraham rose up early in the morning and went.' At the end of this encounter, God said '……now I know'.

SO: Faith Is Not Just Believing God; Faith Is Obeying God to Prove That You Believe Him So As To Commit Him To Perform His Word.

WHEN YOU OBEY HIM, YOU COMMIT HIM TO PERFORM WHAT HE SAID.

Q: Everybody believes God for abundance but how many people are obeying God i.e. fulfilling the conditions required for abundance?

For instance, quoting and confessing Philippians 4:19 all day without doing vs. 15-18 is equivalent to insanity. Everybody believes God for divine health but how many people are obeying the demands of scriptures for divine health? Life and death are in the power of the tongue. Some keep talking sickness and wonder why they are not enjoying divine health. The requirements are: Joshua 1:8-9; Mark 11:20-24; Numbers 14:28 and Proverbs 4:20,21 – 'My son attend to my words and give ear to my sayings let them not depart from your mouth keep them in the midst of thine eyes; for they shall be life to them that find it and health to all their flesh.'

- So you don't become healthy by just talking health but you become healthy by stuffing your spirit man with the truth.

- LIVING THE WORD OF GOD IS LIVING A HEALTHY LIFE. i.e. living on the WORD OF GOD. SO: You are feeding constantly on God's word - exchanging mortality with immortality. Because the words I have spoken to you they are spirit and they are life.

h. So, faith is not just believing God, but attending to, [giving attention to] God's word to produce what you require.

OBEDIENCE IS THE HIGHEST FORM AND EXPRESSION OF FAITH:

Abraham demonstrated that in no unmistakeable terms.

Obedience was the stronghold of Abraham's faith and when you obey the word in truth, because the scriptures cannot be broken God is committed to perform.

Peter said, 'We have toiled all night but at thy word I will let down the net' and they caught a lot of fish and the net brake – obeying God so as to commit Him to perform.

IF GOD SAYS THIS IS THE APPOINTED PLACE – DESERT - JUST OBEY! – It could be far away; far from the city; far from everybody; far from everywhere; what matters is: it's close to God!

It may be contrary to every church growth technique under heaven; it may be a contradiction to every church growth verdict. E.g. John the Baptist located his ministry in the wilderness [desert /dry place] far from the city and yet people came to seek him and what he had for them.

REMEMBER THIS AND NEVER FORGET IT:

a. IF YOU HAVE WHAT PEOPLE REALLY NEED, GOD WILL CAUSE THEM TO MAKE THEIR WAY THERE TO WHERE YOU ARE IRRESPECTIVE!

b. I DON'T CARE WHERE GOD SAYS YOU SHOULD GO; IF IT IS GOD, JUST GO. THAT IS WHERE TO GO.

c. WHERE YOU ARE, IS NOT YOUR PROBLEM; OUR STAND WITH GOD IS WHAT HAS BEEN THE OBSTACLE. IF GOD TOLD YOU, 'GO THERE', THAT'S WHERE YOU BELONG. MOVE NOW and you will experience Isaiah 60:4, 'Lift up thine eyes round about, and see: all they gather themselves together, they come to thee: thy sons shall come from far, and thy daughters shall be nursed at thy side.'

3. FAITH IS NOT, JUST BELIEVING GOD'S WORD, BUT, BEHAVING GOD'S WORD SO AS TO BECOME GOD'S WILL.

Because, God is a God of knowledge by whom actions are weighed. (1 Samuel 2:3)

God weighs our actions to determine his intervention. God watches our actions to determine His involvement or intervention. Hannah was barren and went to Shiloh and the priest told her, her petitions had been granted i.e. go home. She went home and took bread and her countenance was no longer sad. She went home and a year later had the son. She put up the acceptable action or behaviour of joy for God to intervene.

- Joy is a display of confidence in the faithfulness of God.

- The moment you are constantly depressed, you will be cheaply oppressed.

- Whatever God says, there are things to obey and there are things to behave such as 'Rejoice and again I say rejoice; rejoice ever more; rejoice in the Lord always.' Those are all attitudes that must be consciously cultivated. WHY MUST I REJOICE? If God's will is for you to prosper and be in health even as your soul prospers, then joy is a scriptural therapy for health. 'A merry heart doeth good like medicine, but a broken spirit drieth the bones. A man's spirit shall sustain his infirmity but a broken spirit who can bear?' (Proverbs 15:13,15; 17:22; Philippians 3:1; 4:4; 1 Thessalonians 5:16)

- So if you want to become God's will which is divine health, then, you must behave God's word in this regard - which is joy.

- Be comfortable with God knowing that God cannot and will not mismanage your life.

- You don't have a right to existence, it's a privilege; you don't have a right to salvation, it's a gift - a privilege; that's why the psalmist says 'Let everything that hath breath, praise the Lord.' You didn't do anything to stay alive. If He kept you alive, He will do everything else if you let Him.

YOU CANNOT BE GRATEFUL AND NOT BE JOYFUL!

YOU CANNOT BE JOYFUL AND NOT BE PRAISEFUL! And because God inhabits the praises of HIS PEOPLE ………..

YOU CANNOT BE PRAISEFUL AND NOT BE GODFUL!

YOU CANNOT BE GODFUL AND NOT BE WONDERFUL!

SO GRATITUDE IS A COVENANT ATTITUDE!!

Gratitude is a covenant attitude that qualifies you for signs and wonders. It places you in the realm for supernatural happenings.

Every ungrateful person will be joyless. Every ungrateful person will be depressed because what he is saying to God is, 'God, if you know anything, you know I should be higher and better off than this. In other words God you are mismanaging my life.'

Don't entertain depression or discouragement at any time in ministry or life irrespective of what you see or feel or are going through. [The next chapter outlines why a Pastor, Leader or Minister must walk by faith and not entertain or tolerate discouragement]

- Be fully persuaded that God cannot mismanage your life. He can't kill you before your time when you are on a divine assignment. If you don't know the meaning of joy, you are bound to be stranded and cop-out because God cannot survive a joyless environment. If God be for you, who can be against you but if God be not for you, any demon can be against you and floor you.

VALUE GOD'S PRESENCE ABOVE EVERY OTHER THING UNDER HEAVEN!

MAINTAINING YOUR JOY IN MINISTRY

- THE SECRET OF JOY!

'Thy words have I found and eaten and thy words have become the joy and the rejoicing of my heart.' [Jeremiah 15:16]

So, if you are a word-eater not a word-reader, if you become a word-eater, you will have an unending fountain of joy in your life. You can't crash in the plane if you maintain His presence wherever you are with joy unspeakable, full of glory. The devil uses depression to get God off your area because he knows until he gets you out of your Father's house or God off your radar or lenses, he can't strip you naked or torment you the way he wants. Many Christians are cheap victims of depression.

IF SATAN CAN'T STEAL YOUR JOY, HE CAN'T STEAL YOUR GOODS.

Faith therefore is behaving God's word so as to realise God's will in your life; i.e. so as to become His will for you. You can't be healthy no matter how much you confess God's word if you are not joyful. A merry heart services the body, the lungs, the liver, the blood; it services the lungs like medicine but a broken spirit drieth the bones. (Proverbs 17:22)

4. FAITH IS REASONING WITH GOD IN HIS WORD TO DETERMINE YOUR STEPS IN HIS WORD SO AS TO HAVE YOUR DESIRES DELIVERED.

That is why faith is no cheap talk; faith is hard work - you reason with God. Abraham did not stagger at God's promise through unbelief being fully persuaded that what God had promised He was also able to perform. (Romans 4:20-21) To be fully persuaded means you have reasoned through. If God said so, then God is able to do so, because of all this that He did the other time and what He did the other day and based on all that He did, I am now convinced based on these reasons that what God said He will do, He is able to do.

To get to this level, WE NEED MEDITATIONS, A LOT OF IT IN ORDER TO ACCESS THE DEEP THINGS OF GOD!

My father in the Lord talking of the Great Creation Story in Genesis 1 & 2 said: "God moulded clay and breathed into that clay and man became a living soul, one block. So, one breath made man a living soul. So every organ of the body came out of that one breath - the kidney, the lungs, the blood, the water, it's one block, one breath created everything that makes a man. Jesus also said in John 5, 'As the Father has life in himself, so he's given to the son to have life in himself and the Son can quicken whomsoever he will. Then the father said to me as the father hath sent me so send I, you. "Therefore, from God's word we discover that what is coming out of us is life, not carbon dioxide and I have power to give life to anything that is dead by the breath of God from within me. What is coming out of me is LIFE – breath. So, when I breathe on any dead thing it will come to life. Faith is reasoning with God in His word to determine your steps in this word so as to have your desires delivered. So, the life in me by the breath of God in me causes anything that is wrong to be put right; anything that is dead will come to life – COME TO THAT TRUTH!"

FAITH IS NOT A THEOLOGICAL SUBJECT THEREFORE!

FAITH IS A MYSTERY and Scripture says, 'Holding the mystery of the faith in a pure conscience……….'

Therefore Faith is a mystery, and a mystery connotes or contains God's secrets concealed in scriptures. So Faith has divine secrets to it and when we understand these divine secrets, it becomes easy for us to flow in it.

When you operate with such faith, people see what God is doing with you, for you and through you and say, 'This is impossible for the Pastor, for man, for the people but it is only possible for and with God.'

So, you come to a place where the only thing that happens around you is only what God can do.

You get to a point where only what God can do begins to happen around you.

OUR BELIEF AND CONFESSION IN AND OVER OUR MINISTRY HENCEFORTH SHOULD BE: WHATEVER HAPPENS IN OUR MINISTRY WILL BE ONLY WHAT GOD CAN DO!

It does not matter what God says, if it is God, link up with faith and He'll take you there for, Philippians 1:6, 'Being confident of this very thing, that he which hath begun a good work in you will perform it until the day of Jesus Christ:'

5. FAITH IS SEEING IT THE WAY GOD SEES IT. As far as your eyes can see, it shall be given to you – Abraham was taken out and shown the stars in the sky and the stars and the sand on the seashore and told that's how his offspring will be. (Genesis 15:5-6) Scripture says, 'Christ has raised us up together with him and made us to sit together with him in heavenly places.' WHERE? FAR ABOVE!!! ...... far, above, all principalities and powers. (Ephesians 1:20)

- That mentality helps you against any struggle to deal with demon- possessed people. You are far above! Your attitude therefore is: I am not on the same level with you, so I can't be struggling with you!

- SEEING IT THE WAY GOD SEES IT! That is what God says and I see it with Him and as I walk in the consciousness of it, I have unusual victory. There are witches and wizards and all demonic activities but God has positioned us far above them. My father in the Lord asked a witch once: 'Why can't the devil come and help you?' She replied, 'The devil can't come as long as you are here.' Our problem is that of ignorance.

Until you begin to see it the way God sees it, you may remain stranded for life. Satan is not your problem. Your Ignorance is!

You don't have a special problem; you have a special ignorance.

Most people don't have a special problem; their ignorance is what has resulted in what they call a special problem.

You shall not be ignorant anymore.

There is no mountain anywhere. Every man's ignorance is his mountain.

There are no hard places - there are only hard people.

The entrance of his word brings light and that light shines in darkness and darkness comprehends it not. You arise and shine when your light comes – Isaiah 60:1-2.

When you get at the appropriate word, you keep the devil permanently under your feet. I repeat: you keep the enemy permanently under your feet. There is a level of light you possess on a subject that before you say 'Come out', every devil will come out; before you say 'Come out of him', every demonic person will be set free. Jesus had that experience and you will have it too.

SEEING IT THE WAY GOD SEES IT - So that you can keep commanding the same order of results that He commanded.

6. FAITH IS THEREFORE THE MASTER KEY OF DESTINY!

– It is to you according to your faith. Matthew 9:29, 'Then touched he their eyes, saying, According to your faith be it unto you.'

WHAT YOU BELIEVE DETERMINES WHAT YOU BECOME. 'As many as believed in him to them gave He power to become the sons of God.' (John 1:12)

SO, FAITH CONNECTS YOU TO POWER WHICH HELPS YOU TO BECOME WHAT YOU HAVE BELIEVED.

FAITH IS A POWER-POINT THAT CONNECTS YOU TO POWER - THE POWER OF GOD WHICH ENABLES YOU TO BECOME WHAT YOU HAVE BELIEVED.

Romans 1:16, 'I am not ashamed of the power of God, for it is the power of God unto salvation to everyone that believes.'

And when that power flows, you become what you believed - you become what you believed.

MAJOR TRUTH OR REVELATION ON PROSPERITY DISCOVERED EARLY IN MINISTRY:

"God is no respecter of persons but in every nation [no matter where you are or where you came from] everyone that fears him and walks uprightly is acceptable by him;" – Acts 10:34

God is no respecter of persons, race or colour. GOD IS ONLY A RESPECTER OF HIS WORD. GOD IS COLOUR BLIND. FIND THAT TRUTH and walk in the consciousness of it.

You may know many people or many mentors but God is no respecter of persons but in every nation, everyone that fears him and walks uprightly is acceptable by him. 'There is no difference between the Jew and the Greek; for the same Lord over all is rich unto all that call upon Him.' - Romans 10:12

From the truths of these scriptures, you discover that Prosperity is not a citizen of any nation - the same Lord over all is rich unto all that call on Him. In other words: You don't have to become a UK, an American or European Citizen before you enjoy True Prosperity; because Prosperity is not a citizen of any nation.

LISTEN:

YOU ARE NOT DISADVANTAGED,

YOU ARE NOT UNDER-PRIVILEGED;

ALL YOU NEED IS BRIGHTER LIGHT. (Isaiah 60:1-3)

'YOU ARE NOT POOR BECAUSE YOU ARE BLACK; YOU ARE POOR BECAUSE YOU ARE BLIND.' - Bishop Oyedepo

PEOPLE ARE NOT POOR BECAUSE OF THE COLOUR OF THEIR SKIN; PEOPLE ARE POOR BECAUSE OF THE COLOUR OF THEIR MIND.

PEOPLE ARE NOT POOR BECAUSE OF THEIR COLOUR, GEOGRAPHICAL LOCATION OR BACKGROUND; PEOPLE ARE POOR BECAUSE THEY DON'T KNOW, HAVE REJECTED, HAVE FORGOTTEN, DON'T PRACTICE THE COVENANT OR ARE GUILTY OF ALL.

'To be poor in mind is to be poor on earth. Every form of poverty is traceable to poor and idle minds. It takes rich minds to translate into rich pockets and rich hands. Show me a man with a rich mind and I will show you a man with a prosperous hand. Wisdom and riches are companions; wealth is a direct product of wisdom. Everywhere wisdom is mentioned in the Bible, wealth is mentioned as well. Wherever wisdom goes, wealth and riches naturally follow.' - Bishop David Abioye

'GOD IS NOT BLACK, GOD IS NOT WHITE - GOD IS GOD - GOD IS COLOURLESS.' - Bishop David Oyedepo

'When wisdom is at work, nobody makes references to your background - where you're coming from. Everybody forgot that Joseph was a slave because wisdom was at work.' - Bishop David Abioye

'Excellence is the greatest deterrent to racism and sexism.' – Oprah Winfrey

- Faith is not an intellectual fact; Faith is a spiritual force.

- What you believe determines how you behave and how you behave determines what you become.

- Faith is the covenant trigger for the release of the supernatural.

Blessed is she that believeth, for there shall be a performance of the things which the mouth of the Lord hath spoken.

- God wants to revitalise our ministries. As believers, Ministers, Pastors of churches, we must of necessity get back to the base, the root and begin at the beginning. 'Giving all diligence, add to your faith……………'

…… add to your faith………..and Paul also said, above all taking the shield of faith.

WHERE IS FAITH?

Above all! Above All! (Ephesians 6:16)

That's the first.......I know you have the whole armour of God but above all, you need to take the shield of faith …… above all taking the shield of faith wherewith you will be able to quench all the fiery darts of the devil.'

FAITH IS THE FIRST BEFORE AND ABOVE EVERYTHNG ELSE!

7. FAITH IS A SPIRITUAL POWER POINT THAT:

TRANSLATES MORTALITY INTO IMMORTALITY

EXCHANGES THE NATURAL FOR THE SUPERNATURAL

AND TRANSLATES THE HUMAN INTO THE DIVINE

REASON: Mark 9:23 says, 'If thou canst believe all things are possible to him that believeth.'

Mark 10:27, 'With men this is impossible but not with God, for with God all things are possible.'

Therefore: If You Can Believe, Your Status Has Supernaturally Changed.

… YOU ARE NOW ABLE TO HANDLE WHAT ONLY GOD CAN HANDLE!!

YOU HAVE BEEN TRANSLATED FROM MORTALITY TO DIVINITY!

WHEN DIVINITY COMES UPON MORTALITY IT RELEASES AN UNCOMMON PERSONALITY!

'With men this is impossible but not with God, for with God

all things are possible BUT, If thou canst believe all things are possible to him that believeth.' (Mark 10:27; 9:23)

SO, HE THAT BELIEVETH IS NO LONGER A MAN

HE THAT BELIEVETH IS NO LONGER NATURAL

HE THAT BELIEVETH IS NO LONGER MORTAL

SO BIBLE FAITH IS:

- A SPIRITUAL POWER POINT THAT:

TRANSLATES MORTALITY INTO IMMORTALITY

EXCHANGES THE NATURAL FOR THE SUPERNATURAL

AND TRANSFERS OR TRANSLATES THE HUMAN INTO THE DIVINE

Colossians 1:13, 'Who hath delivered us from the power of darkness, and hath translated us into the kingdom of his dear Son:'

- IF YOU ARE LIMITED BY ONLY WHAT MAN CAN DO, YOU ARE NOT IN FAITH. IF YOU CAN ONLY BELIEVE FOR ONLY WHAT A MAN CAN DO, YOU ARE NOT IN FAITH. YOU ARE ONLY IN FAITH IF YOU ARE UNWAVERING IN YOUR TRUST AND CONFIDENCE IN WHAT GOD CAN DO – NO LIMITS – NO BOUNDARIES.

- Be awake and enlarge your coast - it is faith that determines your limits - it is your faith that determines your limits. Bible faith has unlimited gateway for accomplishing our vision. Faith is a mystery and a mystery connotes divine secrets packaged in the scriptures for our mastery. FAITH IS NO CHEAP TALK; FAITH IS HARD WORK! THANK GOD FOR CONFESSIONS; WE MUST DO IT, BUT IF THERE IS NO

SEED IN THE GROUND, RAINFALL IS OF NO BENEFIT TO THE FARMER.

FAITH IS NOT ONLY A CONFESSION [what you say] BUT A PROFESSION [what you do/behave]: The word from your mouth is a way of watering the seed that has been sown in the ground. So, if there is no word in your heart, what you are saying is of no value. It's of no effect. In the school of Prosperity, if there is no seed in the ground, confessions such as, 'I shall prosper or my God shall supply all my need......' is all vanity.

WATERING has no effect except there is seed in the ground.

FAITH IS NO CHEAP TALK; FAITH IS HARD WORK.

So, whatever is the need in your life for God to meet, go first for the seed asking what has God said? How do I see it now? Go first for the seed because without the seed there is no harvest - if you want to have biological or spiritual children go first for the seed, the promise from God's word for children. The word says, '...be fruitful and multiply', believe it, behave it and no devil can stop you from being fruitful; so, first go for the word of God - the word of God is the seed and the words that you speak is the watering that you employ.

IF THERE IS NO SEED, WATERING has no effect.

Don't just believe what He says. DO IT! BEHAVE IT!

SUMMARY:

REVELATION IS: NOT JUST KNOWING WHAT GOD SAYS; REVELATION IS: KNOWING WHAT TO DO HAVING HEARD WHAT GOD HAS SAID. Bible says that Jesus knew in Himself what to do.

- KNOWING WHAT TO DO IS REVELATION. KNOWING WHAT IS WRITTEN IS INFORMATION. INFORMATION IS: KNOWING WHAT IS WRITTEN. REVELATION IS: KNOWING WHAT TO DO, DRAWING FROM WHAT IS WRITTEN"

In the next chapter we will examine why we must ADOPT A ZERO-TOLERANCE FOR DISCOURAGEMENT IN MINISTRY

5

ADOPTING A ZERO-TOLERANCE FOR DISCOURAGEMENT IN MINISTRY

2 Corinthians 4:8-18, 'We are troubled on every side, yet not distressed; we are perplexed, but not in despair; Persecuted, but not forsaken; cast down, but not destroyed; Always bearing about in the body the dying of the Lord Jesus, that the life also of Jesus might be made manifest in our body.'

- It's all about attitude: It's your attitude and not your aptitude that determines your altitude.
- You cannot tailor-make the situations in life, but you can tailor-make the attitudes to fit those situations.

- Discouraged? Just remember that the darkest night did not turn out all the stars.
- 'What happens to a man is less significant than what happens within him.' - Louis L. Mann
- Don't allow discouragement to blight your future.
- Shake yourself from the dust.
- Ego – be strong and courageous. (Joshua 1:1-8)
- Don't compare yourself with others.
- Don't compare your ministry with other ministries. (2 Cor. 10:12)
- Compare yourself with your destiny. (Jer. 1:5-10; Hebrews 10:7)
- Learn to deal with discouragement or it will take you into a deep pit of despair, mountains, caves and strong holds e.g. Judges 6:2, 'And the hand of Midian prevailed against Israel: and because of the Midianites the children of Israel made them the dens which are in the mountains, and caves, and strong holds.' [Order a copy of my book, 'I SHALL RISE AGAIN from www.houseofjudah.org.uk]
- Discouragement makes you hide yourself in caves, and in thickets, and in rocks, and in high places, and in pits. 1 Samuel 13:6, 'When the men of Israel saw that they were in a strait, (for the people were distressed,) then the people did hide themselves in caves, and in thickets, and in rocks, and in high places, and in pits.'
- Discouragement traps you in waste to make you fall by the sword, and places you in an open field to be devoured by the beasts and when it leaves you in the forts and in the caves, its intention is to make you die of the pestilence. Ezekiel 33:27, 'Say thou thus unto them, Thus saith the Lord GOD; As I live, surely they that are in the wastes shall fall by the sword, and him that is in the open field will I give to the beasts to be devoured, and they that be in the forts and in the caves shall die of the pestilence.'

- When discouragement knocks on your door say, 'no'.
- Discouragement makes one glued, negative and only preoccupied with sorrow – so, snap out of it. Jabez did. (1 Chronicles 4:9-10)
- Pastor, what you carry is more than the size of your congregation.
- Pastor, you are more than your congregation. Step up!
- You are more than the size of your congregation and bigger than people's recognition.
- Get rid of the mindset of 'if I work harder' – God is the God of increase. (1 Corinthians 3:6)
- Discouragement is harmful because it makes you ran faster more than is helpful.
- Don't allow discouragement to poison the power of your prophecy. This chapter is to drag you out of your secret discouragement that no one knows about and sees, but you.
- The reason the devil brings discouragement to you is because of the brilliance of what lies ahead of you.
- The greater the discouragement the greater your assignment.
- The greater the discouragement is, is a pointer to the greater things that lies ahead of you.
- Remember: the storms you go through are a measure of your capacity to lead.
- Discouragement will affect your relationship with God.
- Discouragement will steal your joy and will make you read the Bible mechanically.
- Discouragement makes your praise sporadic and your worship plastic.
- Discouragement is a cancer to courage.
- Get understanding – steady yourself. (Proverbs 4:7; 21:16)
- Say to yourself like Job did in Job 19:25, 'For I know that

my redeemer liveth, and that he shall stand at the latter day upon the earth:' Job 13:15, 'Though he slay me, yet will I trust in him: but I will maintain mine own ways before him.'

THINGS TO AVOID:
- Avoid the following things: They tend to be the devil's instruments for discouragement.
- Mental fatigue – find something that gives you a mental break.
- Physical exhaustion produces discouragement. So, have enough rest for your body to allow it to regain its strength.
- Discouraged Pastors poison their potential.
- Find at least two people whose company relaxes your mind.
- Laugh - be happy and joyful - that is why kings have jokers.
- The fact that somebody left you or your ministry does not mean you are dirt. Don't let it get into your heart. (Proverbs 4:20-27)
- Don't let money or number become a prediction of your mandate.
- Write cheques with your mind even if you can't write it with your hand.
- Avoid financial constraints, time-limits and difficulties.
- Fix your marriage – don't have a marriage that makes you drive past your house.
- Make your home a fortress - a safe place where you find peace, joy, contentment and satisfaction.
- Take pleasure in your husband, wife and children – your family.
- Buy a couch that you like sitting in - build yourself a conservatory - get an aquarium to relax you – buy yourself

something you really like.
- Look forward to going home.
- Every minister that does exploits has a strong home-base.
- Avoid chronic sicknesses and bereavements.
- Don't allow declining attendance to be the thermostat of your countenance.
- Don't allow foundational members leaving you to discourage you.
- Thank God for those who come to your church now.
- Thank God for the 200 and the more coming.
- Harsh criticism should not take you out.
- Mind your own business – do not comment on someone's garden or someone's troops – tend yours and supervise yours. (Song of Solomon 1:6; Proverbs 27:3)
- If people point to your past, point to your future.
- If they withdraw your premises, look for another one.
- Have this attitude: there must be somewhere better.
- Enjoy Life – Don't endure life. (John 10:10; 2 Peter 1:3; Romans 8:32)
- Don't compare yourself with another person, another ministry or church – compare yourself to your divine assignment. (Hebrews 9:27)
- Our destinies are about a Divine Clock! Not man's clock.
- Pursue God's divine mandate on your life vigorously.
- Be very focused - **"Be like a postage stamp. Stick to one thing until you get there." - JOSH BILLINGS**
- Nobody can be elevated beyond the level or measure of his **separation, preparation and concentration.** Your separation unto a purpose, a vision or goal in life will give you a consciousness of effective preparation which will earn for you the seat of greatness among the great.
- Adopt Tim Redmond's philosophy on a focussed mind – He said, "There are many things that catch my eye, but

there are only a few things that will catch my heart."
- Many things may catch your eye but don't let everything catch your heart - make sure the things that really catch your heart are your assignment and things that really matter to your destiny.
- Be encouraged – it's not over yet.
- Encourage yourself in the Lord.
- When men say there is a casting down, say, 'There is a lifting up – promotion, elevation, expansion.' (Job 22:29)
- Note those who speak evil of you and invite them for your coronation.

THINGS TO REMEMBER:
- **Ministry is not a journey of trial and error.**
- **Ministry is not a relegation to a life of struggles and suffering.**
- Be educated about the principle before you embark on the ministry.
- Ministry is principally learned.
- Do not sell a divine move to carelessness. Oftentimes, it is ignorance of what you carry that makes you make careless mistakes.
- It is not everything that you are doing which is for public consumption such as the salary you earn or the income the church has. Some testimonies are private and some drives must not be advertised.
- Every dream requires an incubating period. Jesus said in John 16:12, 'I have yet many things to say unto you, but ye cannot bear them now.'
- Not every revelation is for outward consumption.
- You don't tell your close associate certain dreams. If your mouth is loose, God cannot tell you too much.
  Proverbs 21:23 says, 'Whoso keepeth his mouth and his tongue keepeth his soul from troubles.'

Matthew 7:6, 'Give not that which is holy unto the dogs, neither cast ye your pearls before swine, lest they trample them under their feet, and turn again and rend you.'
- A lack of discernment of and discretion with what has been given you can be dangerous. Don't let your enemy know where you are going or he'll go and wait for you.
- Don't build other people ministries at the expense of yours. Song of Solomon 1:6 says, 'Look not upon me, because I am black, because the sun hath looked upon me: my mother's children were angry with me; they made me the keeper of the vineyards; but mine own vineyard have I not kept.'
- Don't get involved with itinerant ministry at the detriment of your church if you are called to Pastor.
- Don't develop a name that is bigger than where you are. Your home base is your priority.
- Don't embark on projects in your church that came from outside. Every generation builds on the previous so build on those that came before you. (Lamentations 3:37)
- Not to have an effective spiritual father is to be ineffective in the move. This move is just starting. (Refer to chapter 8 of my book LEADERSHIP SECRETS - order a copy from www.houseofjudah.org.uk)
- An apostolic mandate means you have ability to duplicate yourself. We are in an apostolic move and the task ahead is great. Ensure that you keep the fire burning. Always set yourself on fire and people will come and watch you burn, catch your fire and run with it to set others on fire.

CHURCH EXPANSION:
- It is those that are sent divinely that triumph divinely and shine brightly and successfully.
- You cannot accept every invitation to speak or else you will blur your vision, blunt your cutting edge and dissipate

your ability to function.
- There can be no transmission without training; make training your overriding watchword and discipleship agenda. Strategize your training – scale it down from young converts to workers, deacons, leaders, ministers, pastors; then evaluate and strengthen.
- Training and feed must be current, practical, relevant and ongoing. Compare where you are, what you are doing with the vision God gave you and beware of competition. Insist on remaining focussed on your race and assignment. (Matthew 6:22)
- Compliment those running; get excited about the successes of others and be genuinely interested in their well-being because what you cannot celebrate, you will never have. Make a vow to yourself that you will rejoice at the success of others. Cover people and see other people's success as yours.
- Whatever you do, don't be happy about the downfall of someone else.
- Search your heart and guard it jealously.
- People under your care must be given a systematic instruction on the areas of your assignment from the scriptures.

TEACH AND ESTABLISH THE 12 PILLARS:
Every church should have pillars of truth taught in series for balanced doctrine and wholesomeness such as:
i. Holiness, Godliness, Righteousness, Consecration & Holy Communion
ii. Faith (The Word)
iii. Vision, Stewardship, Discipleship and Leadership
iv. The Covenant of Kingdom Financial Prosperity [Tithing, Giving, Power to Create and Distribute Wealth]
v. Divine Health, Healing and Deliverance

vi. Mysteries of the Kingdom - The Blood of Jesus, the Name of Jesus, Anointing Oil, Angelic Ministry, Operating In the supernatural, etc.
vii. Prayer, Praise, Fasting and Spiritual Warfare
viii. Family Relationships (Focus on the Family, Marriage, Singles, Youth)
ix. The Holy Spirit [Fruit and Gifts of the Spirit] and the Power of God
x. Evangelism, Missions and Outreach
xi. Wisdom for Success and Victorious Living
xii. The Fear of God and the Incredible power of God's Love

- Feed with substance – give instruction not only inspiration.

6

SECURING YOUR ENVIABLE PLACE IN HISTORY

SELFLESSNESS: THE CAPITAL PRICE TO PAY TO SECURE YOUR PLACE IN HISTORY.
We are going to examine in this chapter the Capital Price for Impactful Leadership and for a ministry with transgenerational impact just like the price that was paid by Jesus, the apostles and the following legends in the kingdom to secure their place in history. e.g. Smith Wigglesworth, Billy Graham, Oral Roberts, Kenneth Hagin, Archbishop Benson Idahosa, Lester Sumrall, T L Osborn, Kathryn Kuhlman, David Yonggi Cho, etc.

John 12:23-26, 'And Jesus answered them, saying, The hour is come, that the Son of man should be glorified. Verily, verily, I say unto you, Except a corn of wheat fall into the ground and die, it abideth alone: but if it die, it bringeth forth much fruit. He that loveth his life shall lose it; and he that hateth his life in this world shall keep it unto life eternal. If any man serve me, let him follow me; and where I am, there shall also my servant be: if any man serve me, him will my Father honour.'

What Jesus was saying was when his hour comes then a price is demanded of him before he can actualize the glory of that hour. We celebrate a lot of prophesies among the Charismatics but we pay little or no attention to the demands that will help us actualize those prophecies.

No pain, no gain. No price, no prize.
Until you have paid the price you cannot earn the prize.

The hour has come for the Son of man to be glorified but verily verily, I say unto you before that glory, there is a price. Except a corn of wheat falls into the ground and dies it abides alone, but when it falls to the ground and dies then it bears much fruit. If any man serves me let him understand this mystery, for that is the only guaranteed access to this glory. Before the glory there is a price to pay. Until a grain of wheat falls down and dies it abides alone. This is the only guaranteed access to this glory. The end time church has been programmed for a season of glory. The most glorious season that the body of Christ has ever seen is dawning on us. The end-time church is destined for a global impact. God has decided to make this glorious. I repeat: Without any doubt the end time church has been programmed for a season of glory - the most glorious season that the body of Christ has ever experienced. The end time church is programmed for a global impact not only that but it has pleased the Lord to make it the turn of people who were not a people. It is our privileged turn to spearhead the next wave of glory that God has packaged for His church but if that is going to be realized we must be aware of the price that has to be paid for that glory to be realized.

It is our turn to spearhead this wave of glory therefore it is our responsibility to pay the price for that glory. Except a corn of wheat falls into the ground and dies it abides alone, but when it falls to the ground and dies then it bears much fruit. If it dies…For us not to fail in this agenda of global impact we must receive the grace to pay the global price. **A global price must be paid to see this global impact. It's a global price for a global impact. People with a global assignment do not keep a normal schedule.** It is our prayer therefore that this section will bring you out of your comfort zone to the zone where you can take your place in history not because you need a name but God has deemed it fit to bring us into the centre of these prophetic days. Everyone who is willing to pay the price will have a testimony to share tomorrow. May you be one of them!

The hour has come for the Son of man to be glorified, but there is a truth that must be in place before the glory can be released. The price is nothing compared with the weight of glory. (2 Corinthians 4:17-18) The glory makes the price to be paid to be as if it was nothing. The price cannot be compared with the weight of glory. That is why scripture says in Hebrews 12:2, 'Jesus who for the joy that was set before him, endured the cross, despised the shame and is now set at the right hand of the throne of God the Father.'

- Whatever is not worth dying for is not worth living for.
- You will only succeed when your assignment becomes your obsession.

Every prophetic agenda is always in need of leadership to be implemented, in order to be executed. God had a plan to bring Israel out of Egypt where He said they will be for only 400 years. But that plan was still on hold after 400 years because God was still looking for a man. They spent 30 years extra in the wilderness because God needed a man before he could bring about his Word. His work among men will have to be effected through human instruments and God said I sought for a man. So in every divine assignment God is always looking for a man to entrust His agenda to him and to bring it to pass through that yielded vessel in line with Amos 3:7, 'Surely the Lord GOD will do nothing, but he revealeth his secret unto his servants the prophets.'

We have discovered that inside every mortal man lies a leadership seed that was placed there from the beginning when God said, Have dominion, take the lead, take command, be in charge, i.e. take charge. So at creation, a leadership seed was implanted in every mortal being. (Genesis 1:26-28) Then in the Abrahamic covenant to which we all belong in the faith (Galatians 3:13-15; Genesis 12:1-3), God further established the reality of this leadership seed because that covenant establishes among many other things that nations and kings will come out of the loins of Abraham which connotes the validity of that leadership seed. So at creation a leadership seed is implanted, in the new covenant a leadership seed is established and in redemption, we are told we are redeemed as kings and priests to reign on the earth. (Revelation 1:6)

We have to engage in scriptural practice to actualize this leadership placement and fulfill our ministry such as adherence to Deuteronomy 28:1, 'And it shall come to pass, if thou shalt hearken diligently unto the voice of the LORD thy God, to observe and to do all his commandments which I command thee this day, that the LORD thy God will set thee on high above all nations of the earth:'

Adherence to vs. 1 entitles us to all the blessings from verses 1 to 14 and many more. So there are covenant practices to engage in to realize this leadership placement and fulfill ministry. It has to be made to bear fruits or produce fruits. So, there is a leader in you that is seeking expression. You carry within your system a leadership seed. Hidden within every follower is a leader waiting to be discovered and released. Prophetically, you are positioned for leadership.

Q: With the above in mind:
a. Why then do we still have a dearth of leadership in the body of Christ?
b. Why are there more slaves in the body than there are kings?

A: It takes a nurturing, self and personal development to bring out that leadership seed to fruition. It takes an organization that is run or led by leaders to become a LEADING ORGANISATION. Every leading organization is largely run by leaders. When you have an army of leaders then you have a leading organization/ministry. It's not a system run by managers, but by leaders.

The CLASSIFICATION OF MANAGEMENT SYSTEMS as we saw in chapter one explains it with clarity - 3 classes
- Managing people or people-management is organization
- Resource management is administration
- Destiny Management is Ministry

That leader in you and the glorious ministry you have will never find expression except certain things give way. The fundamental thing that must give way for the leader in you to come alive is called SELF.

- **WHAT YOU ARE WILLING TO WALK AWAY FROM DETERMINES WHAT GOD WILL BRING TO YOU.**
- **Therefore selflessness can be defined as the capital price for impactful leadership and ministry.**
- **Selflessness - Until the self in you dies, the leader in you cannot come alive.** Inside every man is a leadership seed but multitudes die without ever seeing it come to life. **The death of self is the manure that facilitates the germination of this leadership seed. When self dies it becomes a manure sort of, and that manure facilitates the leadership seed in you.**

SELF and HEAD

Wherever self is enthroned the leadership seed in you is dethroned - one will have to give way to the other. Just as light and darkness cannot co-exist, the same way, self and leadership [headship] cannot stay together; both of them cannot rule at the same time. **WHAT YOU FAIL TO DESTROY WILL EVENTUALLY DESTROY YOU.** Hebrews 11:24-25, 'By faith Moses, when he was come to years, refused to be called the son of Pharaoh's daughter; Choosing rather to suffer affliction with the people of God, than to enjoy the pleasures of sin for a season;'

Moses was a man of affluence in Egypt and a man in pleasures but this passage capitulated his lifestyle saying he chose to suffer affliction with the people of God than to enjoy the pleasures of sin for a season. He abandoned himself for the rescue of the suffering people. When it was time for him to make a choice between God and Egypt, he chose to suffer affliction with his people than the glories of Egypt. He turned his back on what will satisfy his flesh to what will satisfy his calling and purpose of being a deliverer for which he was born. He chose headship in serving God's people to headship over Egypt where he would have been served. He turned his back on the glories of Egypt for the glory of God. That is why we said earlier, - WHAT YOU ARE WILLING TO WALK AWAY FROM DETERMINES WHAT GOD WILL BRING TO YOU.

By walking away from the glories of Egypt, that seed came alive and that seed brought about amazing proofs. He chose. It was not something that was forced on him but rather something that he surrendered himself to. **He chose!** SO SELFLESSNESS IS A CHOICE. It's not a gift or endowment. It is a choice that gives room for the leader in you to come alive. He chose! Inside you is a great leadership seed and great ministry but only you can allow it to come alive or otherwise. Let's look at some scriptural examples. …'By faith Moses, when he was come to years, refused to be called the son of Pharaoh's daughter; Choosing rather to suffer affliction with the people of God, than to enjoy the pleasures of sin for a season;'

NOTE: He refused - He chose - It was an act of his choice - that decision is what gave him his place in history. He chose. That was the choice that gave him his place in history; he was living in the comfort of the palace but he chose. He refused the pleasure of the palace to bury his destiny. He walked away from the pleasures of Egypt and that is what gave him his place in history as the great deliverer of God's people by the finger of God. By his obedience we hear of how Pharaoh and Egypt was silenced; today most have heard of the film 'The Ten Commandments.' Many title holders mistake themselves for leaders/ministers. Many great preachers mistake themselves for leaders. Many title bearers parade themselves as leaders/pastors. YET: True leadership / ministry is rooted in selflessness. That is where true leadership is rooted.
Exodus 2:11-13, 'And it came to pass in those days, when

Moses was grown, that he went out unto his brethren, and looked on their burdens: [he left his own comfort zone] and he spied an Egyptian smiting an Hebrew, one of his brethren; And he looked this way and that way, and when he saw that there was no man, he slew the Egyptian, and hid him in the sand. And when he went out the second day, behold, two men of the Hebrews strove together: and he said to him that did the wrong, Wherefore smitest thou thy fellow?'

HE WENT OUT EVERYDAY, AS A CHOICE - HE CHOSE, HE WAS GOING EVERYDAY despite his comfortable position and comfort zone - he went out every day to see to the welfare of his brethren who were under burdens. He did not have to, but he chose to despite his privileged position. He chose to. He was selflessly committed to the welfare of his people and God concluded, 'I have found a leader.'

SELFLESSNESS IS THE CAPITAL PRICE FOR IMPACTFUL LEADERSHIP - GENERATIONAL LEADERSHIP, LIFE-TRANSFORMING MINISTRY AND FOR SECURING YOUR ENVIABLE PLACE IN HISTORY. GENERATIONAL LEADERSHIP - SUSTAINED LEADERSHIP! This is the reason our mandate as a ministry is RELEASING POTENTIAL, MAXIMIZING DESTINY, RAISING GENERATIONAL LEADERS, IMPACTING NATIONS.

Another example of impactful leadership was Nehemiah. On hearing of the broken down walls of Jerusalem he sat down, fasted, wept, mourned, prayed for many days about the plight of his people and included himself in the confession of sins though he was not there. Why? The news troubled him - he was a selfless man. Bible says he was in the palace, the place of joy, pleasures, fulfillment; he was the king's cupbearer, he had the ears of the king, he was in a high and very privileged position; he was a man of fortune, impact, next to the king - a man of great influence and affluence. Yet he was ready to sacrifice - abandon all that just to see his city rebuilt and the plight and captivity of his people turned around.

HE WAS PASSIONATELY SELFLESS! Bible says he mourned many days in Nehemiah 2:1-3, 'And it came to pass in the month Nisan, in the twentieth year of Artaxerxes the king, that wine was before him: and I took up the wine, and gave it unto the king. Now I had not been beforetime sad in his presence. Wherefore the king said unto me, Why is thy countenance sad, seeing thou art not sick? this is nothing else but sorrow of heart. Then I was very sore afraid, And said unto the king, Let the king live forever: why should not my countenance be sad, when the city, the place of my fathers' sepulchres, lieth waste, and the gates thereof are consumed with fire?

That could have been perceived as rebellious - because he was putting his life and job on the line. As a cupbearer he was always supposed to keep a cheerful countenance in the presence of the king; yet he was saying, 'my life has no meaning; I would rather die than to see this situation continue.'
As a result of his selflessness, favour answered from heaven from vss. 4-9, 'Then the king said unto me, For what dost thou make request? So I prayed to the God of heaven. And I said unto the king, If it please the king, and if thy servant have found favour in thy sight, that thou wouldest send me unto Judah, unto the city of my fathers' sepulchres, that I may build it. And the king said unto me, (the queen also sitting by him,) For how long shall thy journey be? and when wilt thou return? So it pleased the king to send me; and I set him a time. Moreover I said unto the king, If it please the king, let letters be given me to the governors beyond the river, that they may convey me over till I come into Judah; And a letter unto Asaph

the keeper of the king's forest, that he may give me timber to make beams for the gates of the palace which appertained to the house, and for the wall of the city, and for the house that I shall enter into. And the king granted me, according to the good hand of my God upon me. Then I came to the governors beyond the river, and gave them the king's letters. Now the king had sent captains of the army and horsemen with me.' You cannot be truly selfless and be devoid of favour.

Picture of SELFLESSNESS:
- Nehemiah 4:23, 'So neither I, nor my brethren, nor my servants, nor the men of the guard which followed me, none of us put off our clothes, saving that every one put them off for washing.'

- Nehemiah 5:14, 'Moreover from the time that I was appointed to be their governor in the land of Judah, from the twentieth year even unto the two and thirtieth year of Artaxerxes the king, that is, twelve years,'

– I and my brethren have not eaten the bread of the governor. [For 12 years - from 20th year to 32nd year] SELFLESSNESS: the capital price for impactful sustained, generational leadership and a colorful ministry.

CONTRAST BETWEEN SELFLESSNESS AND SELF-FULNESS:

BUT: Nehemiah 5:15, 'But the former governors that had been before me were chargeable unto the people, and had taken of them bread and wine, beside forty shekels of silver; yea, even their servants bare rule over the people: but so did not I, because of the fear of God.'

As a result of their selfishness, greed, avarice, self-fullness, their names never made history. What were their names? Unknown: because they charged the people, they run the people down, but for the fear of God. The governors before him did and so they lost their place in history for gluttony, for greed, for avarice and for self-fullness. Many have sold their birthright for a morsel of meat. May you recover your own today and may you not be found a victim. He continued: Nehemiah 5:16, 'Yea, also I continued in the work of this wall, neither bought we any land: and all my servants were gathered thither unto the work.'

Selflessness gave Nehemiah his place in history. May you secure your place in history like Nehemiah. YOUR STORY IS YOUR HISTORY.YOUR STORY IS YOUR HISTORY.
YOUR STORY IS YOUR HISTORY. Many have no story because of lack of desire to pay the capital price. The price you pay is what determines the worth of your story. Firstly: The price you are willing to pay is what will determine the worth of your story. Secondly: It is the worth of your story that is qualified to become history. [To be written about] It is the worth of your story that qualifies you and gives you a history. Nehemiah died many years ago, yet we are still reading about him. The many governors who took advantage of the people are nowhere to be found and have not been heard of since - there isn't one single historical record of them. That is what happens to selfish, self-full, greedy, avaricious, PEOPLE-USERS who manipulate people and take advantage of others. **You SECURE YOUR PLACE IN HISTORY THROUGH SELFLESSNESS.**

DAVID said, 'I was taking care of my father's sheep and there came a bear and a lion and I run after it.' You don't run after a lion but when you are selfless with a duty to your father's sheep, you are willing to do anything to protect the flock entrusted to you, so that none is harmed, lost, stolen or destroyed - that is what David did. His attitude was: 'I have been put in charge here of this ministry, this church, this flock, this department, this treasury, this office, these people, this house group, this department - my job is to protect what has been entrusted to me. **SELFLESSNESS GAVE DAVID HIS PLACE IN HISTORY.** He saw Goliath defying the armies of Israel and could not tolerate it, saying I'd rather be buried than see this uncircumcised Philistine defying the armies of Israel. (1 Samuel 17) **Generational leadership is rooted in qualitative selflessness.**

WARNING: The Charismatics may never have history because they are not ready to pay any price that secures a person, a system or destinies in history. They are too self-centered, so consumed with themselves and their names. How true Harry Truman's observation was when he said. 'It is amazing how much we can accomplish when no one cares who gets the credit.' Because, many present-day Charismatics want to take the credit for everything in their name, a lot is being left undone and many unreached. When David had an opportunity to destroy King Saul, he refused saying, 'I will not touch the Lord's anointed.' Even when he heard of Saul's death, he broke down and even killed the one who brought the news - Selflessness. Bible says of David that 'After he had served his generation he lay with his fathers.' - Acts 13:36

He did not take advantage of his generation - he served his generation. Don't be committed just because of what God does for you; be committed irrespective, considering it a privilege serving in the kingdom - that should be your motivation. YOUR STORY WILL NOT BE WORTH LISTENING TO EXCEPT IT CONTAINS THE PRICES YOU HAVE HAD TO

PAY IN THE PURSUIT OF YOUR ASSIGNMENT. David served his generation. Can that be said about you and I at the end of our journey that we served our generation?

Let's examine the life of Paul, the Apostle in relation to this subject of selflessness. Philippians 1:21, 'For to me to live is Christ, and to die is gain.'

Philippians 3:7-8, 'But what things were gain to me, those I counted loss for Christ. Yea doubtless, and I count all things but loss for the excellency of the knowledge of Christ Jesus my Lord: for whom I have suffered the loss of all things, and do count them but dung, that I may win Christ,'

DID HE WIN OR NOT AFTER COUNTING ALL THINGS BUT LOSS? Yes, He did. In Galatians 2:20, he said, 'I am crucified with Christ: nevertheless I live; yet not I, but Christ liveth in me: and the life which I now live in the flesh I live by the faith of the Son of God, who loved me, and gave himself for me.'

Two-thirds of the New Testament came through this man - Paul. The leadership in him came alive when the self in him gave way. The leadership in him came alive when the self in him died. The fullness and trans-generational impact of his ministry came alive when the self in him died and is still speaking till date. Jesus said in John 12:24-25, 'Verily, verily, I say unto you, Except a corn of wheat fall into the ground and die, it abideth alone: but if it die, it bringeth forth much fruit. He that loveth his life shall lose it; and he that hateth his life in this world shall keep it unto life eternal.'

The time has come for you to be glorified but except a corn of wheat fall to the ground and dies, you remain the same - but when you die, you bring forth much fruits - you command amazing proofs of leadership and in ministry. So, die to self. It's not about you, it's about Him. That's why John the Baptist prayed in John 3:30, 'He must increase, but I must decrease.' But if it dies - The condition is - this man must die before the glory can come alive - this man must die before he can command proofs.

MANY ARE SO POSITION-SICK THAT THEY ARE CONTRIBUTION-DEAD! Many are so title-crazy that they lose their entitlements in life. What titles do these great men/ women carry? Billy Graham, Kenneth Hagin, TL Osborn, Myles Munroe, Oral Roberts, Lester Sumrall, RW Shambach, Matthew Ashimolowo, George Bush, Barack Obama, Fred Price, David Oyedepo, Kenneth Copeland, Joyce Meyer, Marilyn Hickey, George Adeboye, Mensa Otabil, etc.

HOW DID JESUS EARN THE GREATEST NAME ON EARTH?

The answer is found in Philippians 2:5-11, 'Let this mind be in you, which was also in Christ Jesus: Who, being in the form of God, thought it not robbery to be equal with God: But made himself of no reputation, and took upon him the form of a servant, and was made in the likeness of men: And being found in fashion as a man, he humbled himself, and became obedient unto death, even the death of the cross. **Wherefore God also hath highly exalted him, and given him a name which is above every name: [WHEREFORE - THEREFORE GOD ALSO GAVE HIM HIS PLACE IN HISTORY]** That at the name of Jesus every knee should bow, of things in heaven, and things in earth, and things under the earth; And that every tongue should confess that Jesus Christ is Lord, to the glory of God the Father.'

[WHEREFORE - THEREFORE GOD ALSO GAVE HIM HIS PLACE IN GENERATIONAL LEADERSHIP AND TRANS-GENERATIONAL MINISTRY] HOW? He said let this mind be in you. This is what Paul had to say in Romans 9:1-3, 'I say the truth in Christ, I lie not, my conscience also bearing me witness in the Holy Ghost, That I have great heaviness and continual sorrow in my heart. For I could wish that myself were accursed from Christ for my brethren, my kinsmen according to the flesh:'

I could wish myself accursed from Christ. My conscience bearing me witness; I am not speaking to impress you. So every stride he took to Jerusalem was to reach out to the people, he had continual sorrow, he had great heaviness; that is if my being caught away from Christ will bring them in, let me be caught off. **Even when he had an opportunity to leave, he chose to stay because of the people** as revealed in Philippians 1:23-26, 'For I am in a strait betwixt two, having a desire to depart, and to be with Christ; which is far better: Nevertheless to abide in the flesh is more needful for you. And having this confidence, I know that I shall abide and continue with you all for your furtherance and joy of faith; That your rejoicing may be more abundant in Jesus Christ for me by my coming to you again.'

That was what gave him his place in history till date. But today we have an army of opportunists looking for whom to milk, who to drain, what to take, constantly looking for the next person to take advantage of. WE ARE IN DIRE NEED OF TRUE, SELFLESS LEADERSHIP like Paul who say: 'Behold, the third time I am ready to come to you; and I will not be burdensome to you: for I seek not yours, but you: for the children ought not to lay up for the parents, but the parents for the children.' (2 Corinthians 12:14)

- There are a band of opportunists, prodigal people, seeking only pleasure, not minding the future.
- Position of authority is a responsibility.
- It's not an opportunity to exploit.
- **It does not take a century for God to bless you - it takes a good heart. If you allow self to die today, your place in history will be secured without sweat.**
- Pastors/Ministers/Leaders: Focus on your mission and the assignment not the offerings. Nothing is enough to many pastors and leaders because they have evil eyes. Many leaders don't have a pure heart. Their hearts need a covenant surgical operation so that the evil there can be removed. Paul said my conscience also bearing me witness in the Holy Ghost.

SELFLESSNESS IS PLACING THE LED FIRST.
SELFLESSNESS IS THINKING THE LED FIRST.
SELFLESSNESS is placing the interest of the led far above your interests.

2 Peter 2:1-7 says, 'But there were false prophets also among the people, even as there shall be false teachers among you, who privily shall bring in damnable heresies, even denying the Lord that bought them, and bring upon themselves swift destruction. And many shall follow their pernicious ways; by reason of whom the way of truth shall be evil spoken of. And through covetousness shall they with feigned words make merchandise of you: whose judgment now of a long time lingereth not, and their damnation slumbereth not. For if God spared not the angels that sinned, but cast them down to hell, and delivered them into chains of darkness, to be reserved unto judgment; And spared not the old world, but saved Noah the eighth person, a preacher of righteousness, bringing in the flood upon the world of the ungodly; And turning the cities of Sodom and Gomorrha into ashes condemned them with an overthrow, making them an ensample unto those that after

should live ungodly; And delivered just Lot, vexed with the filthy conversation of the wicked:'

What is God saying here?
When you are selfless, you will not be trapped by covetousness and you will not be part of making a merchandise of the people. Rather, you will be more committed to the welfare of the people more than your own and you will be delivered in the day of accountability and judgment. ADVICE: There is a treasure that has been deposited in you by God to serve your generation - may you not sell it to carelessness or to pleasures and may you not sell your birthright, like Esau but grab it with all your heart. The self in me must die today and the leader in me must come alive. I must not sell my birthright for a morsel of meat. AGAIN: In 2 Corinthians 12:14, Paul said, 'Behold, the third time I am ready to come to you; and I will not be burdensome to you: for I seek not yours, but you: for the children ought not to lay up for the parents, but the parents for the children.'
- For I seek not yours, but you:
- For I seek not your stuff, but rather your welfare/wellbeing:
- For the children ought not to lay up for the parents, but the parents for the children.
    -

THINK ABOUT THIS: How many of us leaders can count what we have laid up in the places where we serve for those whom we serve? How many people can enjoy anything we have laid up for them? What have you laid up for anybody in your life except for preaching: 'Give and it shall be given unto you?' Who else have you given to as a Pastor besides taking from the members? Paul said for I seek not yours, [what belongs to you] but you: [your welfare, wellbeing, progress, success]

Can you say that unequivocally?
Paul could say that because he was a completely selfless man. He continued in Acts 20:33, 'I have coveted no man's silver, or gold, or apparel.'

Paul continued, Acts 20:34-35, 'Yea, ye yourselves know, that these hands have ministered unto my necessities, and to them that were with me. I have showed you all things, how that so labouring ye ought to support the weak, and to remember the words of the Lord Jesus, how he said, It is more blessed to give than to receive.'

SO: WE ARE SUPPORTERS, not consumers or manipulators of church folk. That statement was addressed to pastors - you should labour to support the weak. How many weak folk are you supporting? Are you helping to pick people to church like offering free transportation?

PRACTICAL MINISTRY: As a Pastor/Minister/Leader: Don't be a stylish beggar? Don't make inferences of [indirect references to them] giving to you. If they want to, let them do it of their own accord. Ask for the welfare of the children in your church who may need financial support to help them out. Support some of them, be a father to them: that is how to build the future. Who are you supporting? Which member of your church is praying for you to come to their aid? That is how to secure your place in leadership. There is a leadership seed in you that is craving for expression but self has held it captive. When self loses its grip, then, that seed in you will come alive and will bear fruits, attesting to the leadership grace of God on your life and help you produce maximally in ministry. That's where we are heading.

HOW GEHAZI ENDED HIS MINISTRY:

Through greed, avarice and selfishness. Elisha's grace got Naaman healed and off the spirit of leprosy but he refused to accept any gift from Naaman. But greedy Gehazi, master at taking advantage of people who are ministered to, followed and collected the gifts from Naaman and ended up inheriting Naaman's leprosy and ending his ministry right there. UNTIL SELF GIVES WAY, THE FUTURE REMAINS CLOSED! UNTIL SELF GIVES WAY, THE FUTURE IS NOT IN VIEW! The destiny of Gehazi was closed off because self held him captive - period! His attitude was, 'I will take something from him' - this greedy quest for possessions took from him what he never bargained for as recorded in 2 Kings 5:22-27.

The following scriptures warn us against troubling our own house:
Proverbs 11:29, 'He that troubleth his own house shall inherit the wind: and the fool shall be servant to the wise of heart.'

Proverbs 15:27, 'He that is greedy of gain troubleth his own house; but he that hateth gifts shall live.'

You will not corner troubles to your own house. That is what Gehazi did and his entire family suffered the consequences of his greed.

Proverbs 28:22, 'He that hasteth to be rich hath an evil eye, and considereth not that poverty shall come upon him.'

As someone once said, He who wants to be rich in a day will be hanged in a year. REMEMBER SELFLESSNESS is the capital price for impactful leadership. These biblical historical facts which we have traced should be enough to prop you up because the best of you and in you has still not shown up.

There is something about you - the best in you is yet to come. **Where you are as a ministry is not the reason why you are where you are - who you are is essentially responsible for where you are. Who you are is the reason for where you are. Your positioning is the reason for your present position. So you can change it now! When you adjust your position to be in line with the demands of the truth, the best of you begins to come alive. The best in you will begin to come alive from now as you die to self.**

INTRODUCTION OF THE GREATEST LEADER

When the greatest leader came into this world his introduction was: BEHOLD THE LAMB OF GOD - he was introduced to the world as a living sacrifice. As he came to John he said, 'Behold the Lamb of God that taketh away the sins of the world - BEHOLD THE LAMB OF GOD! BEHOLD THE LAMB OF GOD!'

John 1:29, 'The next day John seeth Jesus coming unto him, and saith, Behold the Lamb of God, which taketh away the sin of the world.'

John 1:36, 'And looking upon Jesus as he walked, he saith, Behold the Lamb of God!'

John 10:17-18, 'Therefore doth my Father love me, because I lay down my life, that I might take it again. No man taketh it from me, but I lay it down of myself. I have power to lay it down, and I have power to take it again. This commandment have I received of my Father.'

STRIVE FOR THIS: I lay down my life. I have power - you have an inbuilt power to decide to be selfless. It is within your power - it is inside you. I have power to lay it down and I have power to take it again - you win the Father's heart because of your selflessness. Selflessness endears you to God. He takes you on because of your selflessness - you lay down your life and take on His agenda. You win God's heart. So, He can say I am pleased with you.

THINK ON THESE: How many of you can boldly declare without a shadow of doubt with a clear conscience that:
- The best of you is invested in the pursuit of your assignment or in your church/ministry?
- That what you are putting in is the best you can afford.
- That the very best of the best is inside the assignment He has placed in my hand till tomorrow.

My prayer is that you will not miss your place in history and that, that captivity of self that is holding you bound and is preventing the leadership seed in you from coming alive will die this hour and forever. Hebrews 11:6 assures us that God is a Rewarder of them that diligently seek him - He - God is the Rewarder. You can't influence God; He is not a respecter of persons and there is no respect of persons with Him. Until God rewards you, there is nothing you are paid that adds to your worth. **Until God rewards you, there is nothing you are paid that will enhance your worth!** It is the reward of God that actually enhances the worth of a man.

Now let us consider the following:
1. **Do you value your destiny?**
2. **Do you value your life?**
3. **Do you value your future?**
4. **Do you value your place in history?**
   - **This is the price to pay to secure it.**

Matthew 20:24-28, 'And when the ten heard it, they were moved with indignation against the two brethren. But Jesus called them unto him, and said, Ye know that the princes of the Gentiles exercise dominion over them, and they that are great exercise authority upon them. But it shall not be so among you: but whosoever will be great among you, let him be your minister; And whosoever will be chief among you, let him be your servant: Even as the Son of man came not to be ministered unto, but to minister, and to give his life a ransom for many.'

He came to give himself for others to live. When you are out to serve, your leadership potential will come alive and your leadership position will be secure. He came to minister and to give his life as a ransom for many. He came for others not for Himself. Live for others, not for yourself. Living for others makes a leader, living for self makes a slave. **CONCLUSION: NO SEED CAN GO TO THE GROUND ON BEHALF OF ANOTHER!**
- **Every seed that must be glorified tomorrow must go to the ground today.**
- So, to secure your own destiny I can't go to the ground for you, you must go to the ground for yourself. Except a corn of wheat fall to the ground and die he abideth alone; so, you must fall to the ground and die.
- **Your place in history will be secured by the quality of selflessness that is involved in your walk with God.**
- **It is your own personal death that will result in your own personal glorification.** Joseph was dead to self in the house of Potiphar and became the envy of the family.
- He was dead to self in the prison; his star shined forth.
- There is nowhere this price does not hold value.
- If he was mindful of self and the now, he would have succumbed to Potiphar's wife and enjoyed better coverage in

the home; but, he was more mindful of the future.
Q: What makes people do what God has not called them to do?
A: SELF
When you are delivered from self, you will secure your place in destiny.

When you are delivered from the captivity of self, you maintain track with divine plan and when you maintain track with divine plan, the oil keeps flowing.

AS WE END THIS CHAPTER PRAY THIS PRAYER:
- Begin to pronounce death on self and its hold on your destiny.
- Begin to pronounce death on self and its hold on your life.
- Self, you must lose your grip off me.
- This leadership seed in me must not go to the grave with me.
- Self, you must lose your grip off my destiny in the name of Jesus.
- Pray in the spirit and secure your hold of your enviable destiny in Jesus' precious name.
- Matthew 19:27-28, 'Then answered Peter and said unto him, Behold, we have forsaken all, and followed thee; what shall we have therefore? And Jesus said unto them, Verily I say unto you, That ye which have followed me, in the regeneration when the Son of man shall sit in the throne of his glory, ye also shall sit upon twelve thrones, judging the twelve tribes of Israel.'

LESSON: So what you forsake today determines where you find yourself tomorrow. 'PAY NOW, PLAY LATER; PLAY NOW, PAY LATER.' - John Maxwell
- What you are ready to give up today for tomorrow will

determine what you can have and walk in tomorrow.
- Live today with tomorrow in mind.
- Sacrifice your present for your future.
- Don't build castles in your stomach; build it out there for all to see and benefit from.
- Legacy! Legacy! Legacy! Leave a positive enviable lasting legacy.

Benefits of Leaving All:
- We have forsaken all. Mark 10:28-31, 'Then Peter began to say unto him, Lo, we have left all, and have followed thee. And Jesus answered and said, Verily I say unto you, There is no man that hath left house, or brethren, or sisters, or father, or mother, or wife, or children, or lands, for my sake, and the gospel's, But he shall receive an hundredfold now in this time, houses, and brethren, and sisters, and mothers, and children, and lands, with persecutions; and in the world to come eternal life. But many that are first shall be last; and the last first.'

There is no one who has left all - made sacrifices, left father, mother, brother, sister, lands houses, etc. who shall not be promoted by receiving a hundredfold in this life plus eternal life….

GENERATIONAL LEADERSHIP TAKES ITS ROOT IN SELFLESSNESS. Vs. 31 - But many that are first shall be last; and the last first.
GRACE TO REMAIN TIRELESSLY SELFLESS - take it today so no one will take your place because ……..many that are first shall be last; and the last first.
- What you forsake today determines where you find yourself tomorrow.
- What you leave or abandon today determines your lot

tomorrow.
- What you give up today will determine what is given to you tomorrow.
- MANY THAT ARE FIRST SHALL BE LAST: meaning they gave up (fainted) and MANY THAT ARE LAST SHALL BE FIRST: meaning they gave up to go up.
- MANY THAT ARE FIRST SHALL BE LAST: meaning they gave up nothing and so got nothing by losing everything and
- MANY THAT ARE LAST SHALL BE FIRST: meaning they gave up everything to get everything.

NEW YORK Times was asked what they thought was responsible for the shift in God's move of the Spirit. Their answer among many other things was: THE KIND OF LEADERSHIP. So God is raising a kind of leadership - a kind that is required to carry out this kind of move.

PRAYER:
- May you find your place in this kind of move and leadership required to fulfill your glorious, impactful, fulfilling trans-generational ministry.
- May someone not take your place.
- May you not be last when you started out as the first.
- May you find yourself in position to be used.
- May your place there not be lost.
- May your place there not be lost to someone else who came after you.
- Lift up your hands and secure grace for this next move.
- Lift up your hands and secure grace for tirelessness in your selfless involvement and pursuit of your assignment
- Grace for continuity, I receive grace from you Lord, for continuity and I receive that today in the name of Jesus Christ.
- From today handle that assignment as if you are the only

one involved in that assignment because God is watching.
- YOUR FUTURE LIES IN WHAT YOU FORSAKE TODAY!
- YOUR FUTURE LIES IN WHAT YOU ABANDON TODAY!
- YOUR FUTURE LIES IN WHAT YOU ARE WILLING TO SACRIFICE TODAY IN EXCHANGE FOR WHAT TOMORROW OFFERS!
- YOUR LOT TOMORROW LIES IN WHAT YOU SUCCEED IN LEAVING TODAY and when that is done faithfully from the heart, diligently, willingly with full commitment then God is committed.

Mark 10:29-30, 'And Jesus answered and said, Verily I say unto you, There is no man that hath left house, or brethren, or sisters, or father, or mother, or wife, or children, or lands, for my sake, and the gospel's, But he shall receive an hundredfold now in this time, houses, and brethren, and sisters, and mothers, and children, and lands, with persecutions; and in the world to come eternal life.'

- The truth is that you have an enviable future, so, don't let the devil rob you of it.
- You have an enviable tomorrow; don't let a temporary pleasure destroy it.
- You have a tomorrow that has a place in history; don't let any devil destroy it.
- Don't sell your future for a morsel of bread or to carelessness.
- The ball is in your court and the grace of God is available to you; do what you please with this God-given opportunity.
- Give thanks!

NOTES:

NOTES:

THE GREATEST GIFT

If you want to take advantage of the contents of this message by asking God to give you power to lead, from which Adam fell, you need to give your life to Jesus Christ. If you have never met or experienced a definite encounter with Jesus Christ, you can know Him today. You can make your life right with Him by accepting Him as your personal Lord and Saviour by praying the following prayer out loud where you are. Pray this prayer with me now:

PRAYER FOR SALVATION: 'O God, I ask you to forgive me for my sins. I believe You sent Jesus to die on the cross for me and confess it with my mouth. I receive Jesus Christ as my personal Lord and Saviour and confess Him as Lord of my life and I give my life willingly to Him now. Thank you Lord for saving me and for making me a new person in Jesus' Name, (2 Corinthians 5:17) Amen.'

If you prayed this prayer, you have now become a child of God (John 1:12) and I welcome you to the family of God. Please let me know about your decision for Jesus by writing to me. I would like to send you some free literature to help you in your new walk with the Lord. So please write to me at the following address:
Correspondence address:
Michael Hutton-Wood,
House of Judah (Praise) Ministries
P. O. Box 1226, Croydon. CR9 6DG. UK.

Or call:
Within the UK:
0208 689 6010, 07956 815 714

Outside the UK:
+44 208 689 6010, +44 7956 815 714

Alternatively Email us at:
Email: info@houseofjudah.org.uk
michaelhutton-wood@fsmail.net

Or visit us at: Website: www.houseofjudah.org.uk
Watch our 24hour internet TV experience
on www.judahtv.org

Other Books And Leadership Manuals By Author

1. A Must For Every New Convert
2. You Need To Do The Ridiculous In Order To Experience The Miraculous
3. 175 Reasons Why You Cannot And Will Not Fail In Life
4. What To Do In The Darkest Hour Of Your Trial [125 Bible Truths You Must Know, Believe, Remember, Confess And Do]
5. Why You Should Pray And How You Should Pray For Your Pastor And Your Church Daily
6. 200 Questions You Must Ask, Investigate And Know Before You Say 'I Do'
7. I Shall Rise Again
8. How To Negotiate Your Desired Future With Today's CurRency
9. Leadership Secrets
10. Leadership Nuggets
11. Leadership Capsules
12. Success Is By Choice And Failure Is By Choice
13. The Dangers Of Procrastination
14. Wisdom Bank

Training Manuals For Impactful Leadership & Effective Ministry

Academy 101 [House Of Judah Academy Curriculum]

Ministry 101

Leadership 101

Kingdom Prosperity 101 From School Of Kingdom Prosperity & Financial Management

Pastoral Leadership 101 From School Of Impactful Pastoral Leadership

Prescriptions 101 - Prescriptions For Fulfilling Your Ministry

To order copies of any of these books, ministry or leadership manuals or for a product catalog of other literature, audiotapes and CDs, DVDs, write to:
Michael Hutton-Wood Ministries,
P. O. Box 1226, Croydon. CR9 6DG. UK.
or [in the UK call] - 0208 689 6010;
[outside UK call] + 442086896010

You can also place your order online as you visit our website: www.houseofjudah.org.uk
or email us at: info@houseofjudah.org.uk; or michaelhutton-wood@fsmail.net

Global Initiatives And Ministries Within The Ministry

TV MINISTRY IN THE UK
Watch Leadership Secrets on KICC TV
SKY Channel 594

Tuesday & Thursday – 3pm & Saturday 5.30pm

Monday-Friday 2pm on FAITH TV
Sky channel 593 & Saturday 3.30pm

LOG ON AND WATCH OUR INTERNET TV PROGRAM on WWW.JUDAHTV.ORG

Anytime - anywhere.

Featuring the:
Teaching Channel
Motivation Channel
Leadership Channel
Family/ Relationships Channel
Upcoming Events/ Products

WATCH US ON YouTube and AUDIO STREAMING EVERY WEEK @ www.houseofjudah.org.uk

Partnering With A Global Ministry Within A Ministry

Michael Hutton-Wood Ministries (The HUTTON-WOOD WORLD OUTREACH MINISTRY) is the apostolic, missions, world outreach, and evangelistic wing of the House of Judah (Praise) Ministries with a mission to God's end time church and the nations of the earth. This ministry was born out of a strong God-given mandate to reach, touch and impact the nations of the earth with the gospel of Christ and bring back divine order, discipline, integrity, godly character, excellence and stability to God's people and God's house. It has a strong apostolic mandate to set in order the things that are out of order and lacking in the church [The Body of Christ] – (Titus 1:5).

Its mission is to save the lost at any cost, depopulate hell and populate heaven with souls that have experienced in full, the new birth, renewal of mind, to produce believers walking in the fullness of their Godly inheritance, divine health, prosperity and authority to take their homes, communities, cities and nations for Christ and occupy till Christ returns. It is to raise a people without spot, wrinkle or blemish. The man of God's passion and drive is that as truly as he lives, this earth shall be filled with the knowledge of the glory of the Lord as the waters cover the sea. His determination is not to rest, hold back or keep silent until he sees the body of Christ established as a praise in the earth. (Numbers 14:21; Habakkuk 2:14; Isaiah 62:6-7)

If you would like to join the faithful brethren and partners of this great ministry by becoming a partner as we believe God for ten thousand partners to partner with this vision prayerfully and financially, ask for a copy of the partners' club commitment card by writing to:

Michael Hutton-Wood Ministries

[Hutton-Wood World Outreach]

P. O. Box 1226, Croydon. Surrey.

CR9 6DG. UK.

Alternatively, you can send a monthly contribution by cheque payable to our ministry or donate online at www.houseofjudah.org.uk or request a direct debit mandate or standing order form from your bankers or us made payable to Michael Hutton-Wood Ministries. Call +44 [0] 208 689 6010 for more details. Philippians 4:19 be your portion and experience as you partner with this work and global mandate. Shalom!

Generational Leadership Training Institute
(The Leaders' Factory)

The Mandate: Raising Generational Leaders, Impacting Nations.

The Generational Leadership Training Institute (GLTI) is the Leadership training and mentoring wing of our ministry with a global mandate to raise leaders with a generational thinking mindset, not a now mentality and to fulfil the Law of Explosive Growth – To add growth, lead followers – To multiply, lead leaders.

This is a Bible College, Leadership Training Institute fulfilling the Matthew 9:37-38 mandate of developing and releasing labourers for the end time harvest. We offer fulltime and part time certificate, diploma, degree and short twelve-week courses in biblical studies, counselling, leadership, practical ministry and schools of prosperity. Its aim is to raise leaders who know and live not just by the anointing but by ministerial ethics, leaders who build with a long term mentality, who live today with tomorrow in mind. The mission of this unique educational and impartation institution is to transform followers into generational leaders and its motto is to raise leaders of discipline, integrity, godly character and excellence - D.I.C.E.

For correspondence, full time, part time, online courses, prospectus, fees and registration forms for the next course, call 0208 689 6010 or write to the Registrar, GLTI, P. O. Box 1226, Croydon. CR9 6DG. UK or from outside UK call +44 208 689 6010.

Additional information can be obtained from visiting our website www.houseofjudah.org.uk looking for THE LEADERS FACTORY.

Log on to www.judahtv.org for Leadership Secrets and other teaching.

This is a hutton-wood publication

Leaders Factory International

MANDATE: 'In the business of training, developing and raising and releasing more leaders and leaders of leaders.'

'Leaders must be close enough to relate to others, but far enough ahead to motivate them.' – John Maxwell

'You must live with people to know their problems, and live with God in order to solve them.' – P. T. Forsyth

If you, your organisation, college, university, business or church would like to invite Dr. Michael Hutton-Wood for a Motivational-speaking, mentoring or leadership coaching engagement or to organize or hold a Leaders Factory seminar or conference, Leadership Development or Human Capital building seminar, Emerging leaders seminar, Management seminar, Business seminar, Effective people-management, Wealth-creation seminar or training for your workers, leaders, staff, ministers, employers, employees, congregation, youth, etc. you can contact us on 0208 689 6010 [UK] +44208 689 6010 [OUTSIDE UK].

Alternatively by email at:

- info@houseofjudah.org.uk

- michaelhutton-wood@fsmail.net

or leadersfactoryinternational@yahoo.com

VISIT our website: www.houseofjudah.org.uk

You can watch our internet TV experience www.judahtv.org [Maximizing Destiny and Leadership Secrets].

This is a Hutton-Wood publication

MANDATE:
Releasing Potential - Maximizing Destiny
Raising Generational Leaders - Impacting Nations

SIMPA
SCEPTRE INTERNATIONAL MINISTERS & PASTORS ASSOCIATION

This covenant mandate comes from Genesis 49:10: 'The sceptre [of Leadership] shall not depart from JUDAH, nor a lawgiver from between his feet, until Shiloh come and unto Him shall the gathering of the people be'

Other covenant scriptures backing this mandate are: Isaiah 55:4 & Titus 1:5. We have a leadership assignment to RAISE GENERATIONAL LEADERS TO IMPACT NATIONS BY DISCOVERING MEN/WOMEN AND EMPOWERING THEM TO RELEASE THEIR POTENTIAL TO MAXIMIZE THEIR DESTINY.

SIMPA is a multi-cultural fellowship/network of diverse Christian leaders, pastors and ministers that recognize the need for fathering, covering and mentoring. The heartbeat of the man of God is to pour into the willing and obedient what has made him and keeps making him from what he's learnt from his father in the Lord, his teachers and mentors which is working for him and producing maximally. He said: 'I discovered this secret early: Not to learn from or follow those who make promises but from those who have obtained the promises, proofs and results. REMEMBER: YOU DON'T NEED TO MAKE NOISE TO MAKE NEWS. SO: FOLLOW NEWS-MAKERS NOT NOISE-MAKERS!'

These are a few of the mindsets of the man of God:

When the students are ready, the teacher will teach.

'YOU NEED FATHERS TO FATHER YOU TO GROW FEATHERS TO FLY.' – Bishop Oyedepo

'Without a father to father you, you can never grow feathers to fly and go further in life, than they went and accomplish more than they did.' – Michael Hutton-Wood

Don't raise money; raise men and you'll have all the money you need to accomplish your assignment.

There is no new thing under the sun – King Solomon

What you desire to attain, become and accomplish in life, someone has accomplished it – find them, follow them, learn from them, sow into them and their resource materials and you will do more than they did and get there faster.

Teachers, Trainers, Mentors and Fathers give you

speed/acceleration in every field of endeavour.

Isaac Newton is known to have said the following:

'If I have seen further it has been by standing on the shoulders of those who have gone ahead of me.'

Variant translations: 'Plato is my friend, Aristotle is my friend, but my best friend is truth.'

'Plato is my friend — Aristotle is my friend — truth is a greater friend.'

'If I have seen further it is only by standing on the shoulders of giants.'

Without a reference you can never become a reference.

If you don't refer to anyone no one will refer to you.

Who laid / lays hands on you and what did / do they leave behind?

This is not a money-making venture but rather about covering and empowerment for fulfilment of destiny and assignment within time allocated.

The goal of SIMPA is to spiritually cover, strengthen, equip, empower, train, mentor and encourage and lift up the arms/hands of both emerging and active [full and part time] pastors, ministers and leaders and by so doing release them to fulfil their respective assignments both in ministry and the market place.

IF YOU WOULD LIKE TO BE A PART OF SIMPA, ASK FOR A REGISTRATION FORM & PAMPHLET FROM OUR INFORMATION DESK in House of Judah or email info@houseofjudah.org.uk or call [in the UK] 0208 689 6010 [outside UK call] + 44 208 689 6010 requesting for SIMPA registration form and pamphlet.

– SEE YOU ON TOP!

Shalom! – Bishop

PARTNERSHIP:

In the UK write or send cheque donations to:
Michael Hutton-Wood Ministries
P. O. Box 1226 Croydon. CR9 6DG. UK.

In the UK Call: 0208 689 6010; 07956 815 714
Outside the UK call: +44 208 689 6010;
+ 44 7956 815 714
Fax: +44 20 8689 3301
Email:
info@houseofjudah.org.uk
michaelhutton-wood@fsmail.net
leadersfactoryinternational@yahoo.com
judah@houseofjudah.freeserve.co.uk
Or visit or donate online at our secure
WEBSITE: www.houseofjudah.org.uk

Watch our 24 hour internet TV experience by logging on anywhere - anytime @ www.judahtv.org

BOOKS AND LEADERSHIP MANUALS
BY BISHOP MICHAEL HUTTON-WOOD

What is Ministry

My Daily Bible Reading Guide

Leadership Nuggets

175 Reasons Why You Cannot And Will Not Fail In Life

I Shall Rise Agian

Leadership Capsules

What To Do In The Darkest Hour of Your Trial

Generating Finances For Ministry

TRAINING MANUALS FOR IMPACTFUL LEADERSHIP & EFFECTIVE MINISTRY

Please log on to **www.houseofjudah.org.uk** for more information

OTHER BOOKS BY THE AUTHOR
- BISHOP MICHAEL HUTTON-WOOD -

Why You Should Pray for your Pastor And For Your Church Daily

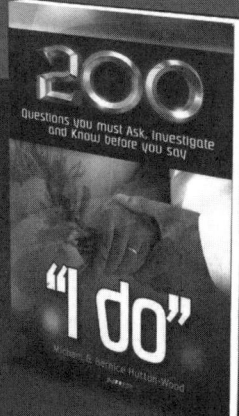

200 Questions You Must Ask, Investigate And Know Before You Say I Do

A Must For Every New Convert

How To Negotiate Your Desired Future With Today's Currency

Leadership Secrets

You Need To Do The Ridiculous In Order To Experience The Miraculous

Please log on to
www.houseofjudah.org.uk for more information